Youth in Exodus

About the author

Geraldine Witcher has spent her entire adult life working with children and teenagers in both a secular and church environment. A qualified teacher, specialising now in specific learning difficulties, she has taught in the state and private sectors both in primary and secondary schools. She has been a Crusader leader, and has led Sunday schools and Youth Groups, and run children's holiday clubs. She has been a congregational leader in a family orientated community church and is involved in counselling and teaching young people in Eastern Europe. She has been a writer of Scripture Union's Education in Churches (SALT) material for many years, and, in addition to magazine articles on child and youth related subjects, is the author of eight books of stories for children and editor of one book of assembly outlines for use in Primary Schools. She is also the mother of two adult children who are both strongly committed Christians.

About Highland Books

From our website, www.highlandbks.com, you can find out more, download our catalogue, or see if we have posted any errata. Conversely, you can tell us about errors at
 errata@highlandbks.com
or send appreciations to authors@highlandbks.com.

Youth in Exodus

The church must stop the haemorrhage of its young people and banish the generation gap from God's kingdom

Geraldine Witcher

Highland

Godalming, Surrey

First published in 2002 by Highland Books, Two High Pines, Knoll Road, Godalming, Surrey GU7 2EP.

ISBN: 1-897913-64-8

259.23 WHI

Printed in the UK by Bookmarque, Croydon.

Contents

1. Starting Point 7

2. The Status Quo 11

3. The Facts 19

4. Understanding Covenant. 33

5. Generational Promises. 48

6. Regeneration – Trauma or Growth? 59

7. God and Children 72

8. Living inside the Covenant. . . . 85

9. What the Children Need 103

10. What the Teenagers Need 116

11. Aspects of Life with God 128

12. Church in Community 145

13. Churches that Work 161

14. The Way Forward 168

Chapter One

Starting Point

The Archbishop of Canterbury, George Carey, spoke these words to the World Council of Churches in Zimbabwe in 1998: 'Our mission is under attack ... In some sections of the Western Church we are bleeding to death.'

I do not believe that he thinks for one minute that the western Church *will* bleed to death, but the very fact that he said such a thing shows how serious the situation is. The crisis in the church today is the theme of many books at present available. In microcosm the same feelings were expressed in a very different way to me, and it is the juxtaposition of the local with the wider picture, that convinced me that this book needed to be written.

While my children were growing up my husband and I were leaders in a new church on a housing estate on the outskirts of Reading. During that time we were very involved in children and young people in many different ways, being involved in youth groups, Bible clubs, a drug rehabilitation centre, teaching and of course our own children and their friends. Having spent seventeen years in this church, we moved to another – a lively charismatic Baptist church with five congregations and dynamic leadership. Then something strange happened; over and over again we were asked what we did to have such strongly committed children (then 16 and 18). 'How will I cope when mine hit the rebellious teens?' I was asked. 'What can I do to make mine turn out like yours?' another mother asked. The same question from many different people in many different ways; 'How come your children have come safely through their teenage years and become such attractive and strong Christians?' 'But we didn't do anything – only believed,' was my mystified reply. What had we done? I hadn't thought my children were anything special; in the church they grew up in, strong vibrant actively Christian teenagers were the norm. What had we got right? Had we done things differently, and if so what?

In the end I put it down to serendipity and God's grace. Serendipity because somehow, in that church they grew up in, we found a 'formula' that worked. Looking back on it, it was biblical and therefore secure. Grace, because we were all just ordinary Christians depending on him for our families and our future. But the question remained, and this book is the long form of the answer. This is what we did. It worked for my children and many others and my prayer is that some of what is contained here will help many of us, church leaders and parents alike, to create an environment where many more children grow into strong faith easily and naturally.

I don't want to be part of a church that is bleeding to death. I don't want to imagine a church without young people in it. I don't want to be like the elderly congregation we joined on holiday in the West Country whose prayers told God how dreadful the world was these days and how much better the old days were. They finished by calling down vengeance on this godless younger generation – yes really!

There is a sense in which the church in Britain is in imminent danger of running out of lifeblood out at the beginning of this twenty-first century. But Jesus said he would build his church – it is meant to *grow*. So it's time we stopped pretending and admitted that it *isn't* and started doing something about it. The place to start is with our own children – the children in our families and in our churches. Parents and church leaders need to work together to guard and develop this precious resource – the church of today and tomorrow. My hope is that this book will take its part in helping that to happen.

Part one

Bleeding to death?

The church in the West has been said
to be haemorrhaging; its young
people and children are draining
away from the church.

Chapter Two

The Status Quo

I was talking to a member of our church the other day, when she mentioned her children. I didn't know she had any; they are never seen in church and haven't been in the five years I have been here. 'Oh, yes,' she said. 'I have two boys, teenagers. No they don't come to church now. They used to, but they stopped. It's inevitable isn't it? I guess they'll come back – in God's time.'

How sad! (In both the new and the old interpretation of the word!) *Why* is it inevitable that our teenagers give up on church? And *will* they come back? The statistics make it seem very unlikely. Once lost to the church, they are usually lost for good. Whatever makes us think it's God's plan that our enthusiastic children turn into rebellious teenagers and waste years of growing up with their backs firmly turned to him? The saddest thing about this conversation was that she, like so many other Christian parents, accepted this state of affairs as the norm, the way things are and the way they should be. The church doesn't seem too worried either; we celebrate our young missionaries, and rejoice when one or two are baptised but don't remember the many children of the church who no longer attend and who have gone their own way.

It is time we looked at the facts. The facts tell us that the church in Britain has lost its young adults, the so called Generation X, is losing its teenagers, and is beginning to lose its preteens. Church is seen as an optional add-on to life, not a vital part of it. The faith of the church, our faith, has been judged as irrelevant, out of date, nothing to do with them. As they grow up, our children are discarding belief in God in the same way as they grow out of Father Christmas and the tooth fairy, as stories for children which have no relevance in the adult world they are growing into. Their world is full of next month's fashions to buy, computer games to play, mobile phones to chat on and night-clubs to dance and socialize in. Their spiritual life is centred on their horoscopes, fengshui, crystals and self-help. They have no room for the God of the Bible in all this. They have left the church and gone on to more exciting things.

This haemorrhaging of our youth is as dangerous for the health of the church as uncontrolled loss of blood to the body. If we keep losing the next generation, death will inevitably follow. At the Swanwick conference in England in March 1999, Archbishop George Carey spoke these ominous words; 'The church is one generation away from extinction.' It is possible to argue that this has always been the case, but there is now a missing generation, generation X, which is not in a position to hand down the truths of the church because it is not a reality any more in their lives, even if they began with Sunday school. We all know that any species that is only one generation away from extinction is very severely endangered indeed and needs help urgently to prevent total disaster. Reproduction is the only way to pull back – and we are consistently failing to reproduce.

But it doesn't have to be this way. This is not how God designed it. Jesus told Peter, 'upon this rock, I will build my church.' [Matthew 16:18] The church was God's idea and throughout the ages it has persisted, sometimes weak and corrupt, sometimes strong and vibrant, but always transmitting faith down the generations. Until now. Yet God does not leave us helpless, and he is not impotent in the face of the changes that are coming ever more rapidly into the world in which we live. The Gospel is still the good news. There are still families where faith is handed down to the next generation, time after time. There are teenagers whose parents stand back in wonder and gratitude at the strength of their faith and the things they are doing with and for God. I know; I'm one of them. If there are some, then there can be more. Having looked at, and talked to many families of both kinds, having discussed with church leaders and ploughed my way through charts and diagrams by the pageful, I still believe that we can make a difference to the number of children who turn their backs on the traditional faith along with their childhood. We can fight back from extinction.

But only if we open our eyes and face the facts. If we continue to hide from unpalatable facts, and pretend that all is well, we are like someone with cancer who could be healed but refuses to go to the doctor because he does not want to hear the death sentence. The church in the West has lost sight of some of the truths about God and how he deals with mankind; we have bought into ungodly views of childhood and we have forgotten that our God is infinitely powerful and infinitely loving. We have conformed so much to the cultural climate in which we live that we are virtually indistinguishable from those outside the church. We have watered down the demands of Jesus so much that there is no challenge and no excitement left in them. We have forgotten that understanding and interacting with the society we are in is vital to influencing it.

People's basic need for community and relationship is growing as everything else gets globalised. Children, growing up surrounded by the virtual reality of Internet chat rooms and the World Wide Web, still need people to relate to. Whether we like it or not, technological and economic globalisation is here to stay. But while teenagers from the North of Scotland to the streets of Beijing wear identical jeans, listen to the same music and eat the same Mcfood, they also have the same needs for love and significance. They are so different from their parents that they seem like a different species; the world they are growing up into is one that our generation could not even imagine at their age, yet the basic human needs do not change. They live in the global village but they need a village type community, somewhere where they count as individuals, not just as one of the masses. Church could be the place that provides that security but no one thinks to look there for it. We are seen as an insignificant minority, who, living as we do, in a largely self-imposed ghetto, are out of touch with reality. We are not of course; we are in touch with *real* reality in a way that other people have no idea is even possible. But we can, and often do, give the impression of being afraid of what is happening in society and negative about everything that is going on, especially when it concerns the younger generation. And yet, as Christians we are surely agreed that church – the people, not the building – is the only place where unconditional love, true forgiveness, real creativity and the Holy Spirit can be found. Our young people desperately need all of this. It has been said that church needs to find a new form, one which works in a post-modern society. But there are basics which, whatever the form, remain constant. God's love for mankind is constant. His indwelling Spirit is as powerful as he had ever been. Jesus is still building his church. He still wants us to live kingdom lives. But we need to work out how this all applies to us, as people and as churches at the beginning of the third millennium. We will only be able to achieve this new form of church when we have a true understanding of God's commitment to his people, and a determination to live in a way that demonstrates the reality of that commitment.

If we began again to see that church and mission are inextricably entwined; if we understood that Kingdom living is not an optional extra; if we knew how to love God perfectly and each other unconditionally; if we understood and demonstrated what holiness is; if we learnt how to create true community; if we could do all these things, or even begin to do some of them, our children would be fighting to stay a part of it all. Yesterday I was speaking to a twenty year old, in the process of training (alongside other young people) for missionary work with Youth With A Mission; she made the comment, 'When you've seen it for yourself, and you know it's real, it's very difficult to turn away from it.'

The life of the Kingdom lived out in everyday relationships is compelling; this young lady saw the reality of Jesus in her parents' lives, and 'fell in love' with him for herself. We have to learn to duplicate her experience for all the others – the ones who find the pubs and clubs more exciting.

When our son was about eight, he was given a kite. It was the most wonderful kite, not least because Granny and Granddad had brought it all the way from California for him. It was bright red and had a tail fully fifteen feet long and it was made of bright shiny stuff that looked and felt like cellophane, but must have been much stronger. Two children and Dad took the kite to the local park to try it out. As is the way of kites, it took a lot of failed attempts, bumping along the ground, diving suicidally downwards once airborne, but eventually it flew – straight into the nearest tree. And stuck there, right at the top, completely entangled. Fifteen feet of tail can do a lot of tangling! There was no way that kite was coming free. But David knew what to do – and so they prayed. The children had complete faith that God would rescue the kite; Dad was not so sure. But a strong, single gust of wind came, blew around the tree, and freed the kite, to Dad's amazement and the children's confident joy.

For many of us life in general, and church life in particular, indeed seem the kind of hopeless tangle that a kite in a tree represents. Just how do we sort out the basics from the cultural add-ons? What is it that makes church, church? What is it that makes faith attractive to young people? Has the church in the west got into the habit of looking at society, looking at the life our teenagers lead, looking at all the difficulties, and saying, 'Nothing can be done,' and forgetting that God is involved in the picture? If we really understood how committed God is to humanity, and how to live out the reality of that commitment, it would make a difference. It has to. God, who freed the kite with a gust of wind, can blow the whirlwind of his Spirit into the church and free and transform it, so that our children will stand amazed at his intervention in their lives.

Look at the way Jesus lived. What did he do most of? Eating meals and going for walks with his friends! Talking – lots and lots of talking. Meeting people and changing their lives. Don't you think his lifestyle was compelling – freedom from worry about possessions, unconditional acceptance of people as they are, enabling them to become what they can, enjoyment of people, reliance on the goodness and nearness of a loving powerful Father. Wouldn't our children thrive in such an environment? Wouldn't we? Wouldn't the church? We need a bit less of Dad's 'It can't be done' and a lot more of the children's total faith that God is in control and he cares!

When the church models Kingdom living, as Jesus demonstrated it, and takes the teaching of the epistles on relationship and lifestyle seriously, and knows and trusts the promises God has made to his people; when we live all this out in daily response to God's revelation of himself, then I believe we will see the haemorrhaging stop, and our children begin to grow up into the heritage that is theirs, without the wilderness years having to come first. The Israelites, wandering in the desert for forty years, dying off one by one, knowing they would never get into the Promised Land themselves even if their children did, must have been kicking themselves whenever they remembered that Caleb and Joshua said crossing the Jordan and taking the land was possible. It was their fear and their lack of belief in God's promises, and their misunderstanding of his purposes for them, that kept them out of that 'land flowing with milk and honey'. Our promised land may be our children for the Lord; don't let's condemn them and us to forty years wandering in the desert because we don't believe God's promises.

Chapter Three

The Facts

Barak was terrified. Down on the plains, as far as his eye could see, there were people. On his plains, the plains of Moab, they should have been Moabites. But they weren't. These were Israelites – thousands of them, all heading for his country. Barak knew they had killed the Amorites and he was terrified that he was next on their list. So he sent envoys, and money, to Balaam. Balaam was a prophet who listened to God. Barak knew this and wanted Balaam to curse the Israelites. Balaam refused twice, because God told him the people were blessed, but at last God told him he could go with the princes of Moab. So on this fine morning Balaam was riding his donkey towards the Moabite king. It was a good donkey; it had always carried him faithfully and obediently wherever he wanted to go. Balaam thought he was doing the right thing; he was going with Barak's men, and maybe now God would let him curse the Israelites. Being in the pay of the Moabite king, he naturally did not want these invaders taking over the land, even if they were blessed by God.

But suddenly the donkey swerved off the road and into a field. Balaam beat her and drove her back onto the road. Then, passing along a narrow stretch of road between two walls, the donkey stopped again and cowered against one of the walls, crushing Balaam's foot against the stone. Angry and in pain, he beat her again. She started forward again, but then suddenly lay down in the road. By this time Balaam was furious and beat her a third time. At which point the donkey started talking to him! What the donkey knew, and we know if we have read the story in the Bible, [Numbers 22], was that there was an angel blocking the way! Balaam beat the donkey when she stopped because he didn't see what was really happening!

It's a very strange story, isn't it? We may wonder why it is there in the Bible. But, in a simple way, we in the church in the West can be a bit like Balaam. Not that we all go around beating donkeys, I hope, but that we fail to see what is before our eyes. The danger in a serious haemorrhage is that often there is not as much pain as there might be for a far less serious condition. Blood draining away can be a gentle experience during which it is not immediately apparent there is something wrong. It is possible that the church, and Christian families are, like Balaam, going the wrong way because we are not seeing the obvious.

It is easy to look at a church congregation and think all is well. After all, there are noticeable spaces left when the children go out to Junior church or whatever their 'club' is called. There is young Sarah, who plays her flute so nicely with the worship group, and John who makes such a lovely noise (!) on the drums. There are always lots of children running round and getting in the way afterwards when the adults are trying to drink their coffee and have a chat. The teenagers put on such a lovely play at Christmas. All is well. Until we look at the picture more carefully. Until we remember the little ones whom we don't see any more now that they have gone to secondary school and grown more independent. Until we realize how many children have stayed at home, how many teenagers are in the nightclub or pub rather than in church with their parents on a Sunday evening.

I did a survey of our church to find out which and how many children stopped coming to church, at what age, and how involved their parents were with the life of the church. Our youth pastor told me that we actually only have about half the children of the adults in our church involved in any way, however spasmodically, in the youth activities, and that many of them drop out at sixteen or so, because of the pull of the 'world'. So 50% of our children are not involved in their parents' church through their teenage years, and another 20% drop out around 18 when they leave for further education. If not now, when will they ever enter a church building? I also did a count at a typical Sunday morning service: of 28 sets of parents in church that day who had teenage or twenties children, 11 families had children who no longer attended church at all.

I am very grateful to Peter Brierley and the Christian Research organisation, which did surveys of the whole country to find out the same thing nationwide! Their findings are quite horrific. In England in 1980, taking all denominations, 10.2% of the adult population were regular church attendees. By 1999 that proportion had dropped to 7.7%. When we realize that in this survey adult is taken as over the age of 15, we begin to see that a lot of our teenagers are voting with their feet.

Over the same period Sunday school attendance has dropped from 9% to 4% of the relevant population. In real terms this means that 200 children under fifteen are leaving the church every week! (Or it did when I first wrote these words. By the time you read them, the rate may even have speeded up.) The older children will presumably be making that decision for themselves, but this also reflects the fact that it is mostly the younger adults who are leaving church, taking their children with them in some cases. The figure for all people under the age of thirty leaving the church in England is 1000 per week. How long can this go on before the church stops being viable as an organisation?

So far these figures have been compared with the population as a whole. When you turn to analyse percentages of the church going population only, we see more worrying trends.

The proportions of churchgoers by age sees 15-19 year old as the smallest, being only 6% of the total, (under15s making up 19%) and young adults (20-29) as second lowest, being 9%. (Figures taken from the Christian Research 'Religious trends 2000/2001 edited by Peter Brierley) Already low in numbers, these are also the age groups which are shrinking most rapidly. The church is dying 'from the bottom up'.

I don't know about you, but as far as I am concerned, figures and statistics tend to make me feel as if I am going cross-eyed and brain dead. So

Sunday attendance by age-group, 1979-1998
(in thousands)

Numbers derived from tables published by christian-research.co.uk website and their publication Religious Trends

	Under 15	15-19	20-29	30-44	45-64	65 or over	TOTAL
Churchgoers 1979	1,416	490	598	870	1,088	979	5,441
" " 1989	1,177	337	481	809	1,043	895	4,743
" [A] 1998	717	211	327	647	886	928	3,715
[B] UK pop. 1998	11,607	3,641	7,806	13,042	13,571	9,223	58,889
Distribution of ages as percentages							
[A] Churchgoers	19%	6%	9%	17%	24%	25%	100%
[B] UK population	20%	6%	13%	22%	23%	16%	100%
[B / A] deficit/surplus	-2.1%	-8.9%	-50.6%	-27.2%	+3.4%	+37.3%	

(last row means church must grow 20-29 group 50.6% just to reach the same proportion of this age group as church represents of the whole population)

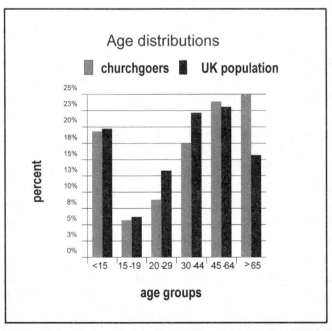

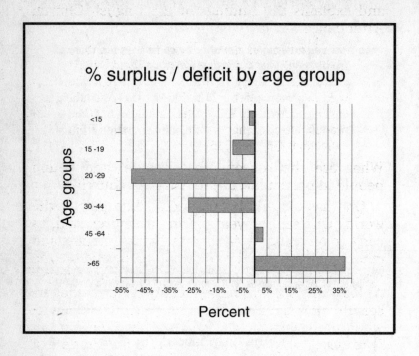

% surplus / deficit by age group

here are two quotes, which sum up in words what the statistics tell us with figures.

> Within two decades the entire Western Church is likely to see even more rapid decline because of our inability to keep and reach the young in our Western Churches.'

So says Tom Sine in *Mustard Seed Versus McWorld*. He says that wherever we look in the church throughout the English speaking world, the under thirty fives are the missing generation.

Peter Brierley puts it in even starker terms in his book, *The Tide is Running Out* which documents and explains the findings of the English Church Attendance Survey;

> I am a statistician, not a theologian. The numbers in this book show a haemorrhage akin to a burst artery. The country is littered with people who used to go to church but no longer do. We could well bleed to death. The tide is running out. At the present rate of change we are one generation from extinction. [op. cit. p236]

What are the reasons that people, and young people in particular, are leaving the church?

One has already been stated – 'the pull of the world'. One sixteen year old in our church said, ' I can't go on being two things – what my parents and church want on Sunday and wanting fun and life the rest of the week. I'm going out to experience things!' At least this one was honest; many of our teenagers seem to manage a dual life until they leave home, when they drop the Christian bit. In *Gone but not Forgotten* Philip Richter and Leslie Francis list reasons such as going for the wrong reasons, pretending to be something I'm not, lifestyle incompatibility, lack of relevance, lack of challenge or vision, hypocrisy and trivialisation of religious matters by the adults, not being valued and not having needs met. These are all cited as frequent reasons for leaving the church. It seems we are not giving them real life; they are leaving the church to find that elsewhere.

What about my friend's pious hope that her boys would one day return to church and commit themselves to the Lord? Is there any reality to it? The figures seem to imply that her hope is no more than self-delusion. Traditionally in past generations the proportions returning when they marry and have children seems to have been quite high, but we cannot rely on this continuing. This generation growing up now is the first which has no basis of spiritual knowledge or tradition of church-going or worship in school. As Douglas Coupland puts it – starkly, the only words on the page, in his sad, haunting book, *Life after God:* 'You are the first generation raised without religion.'

New parents have many other calls on their time, not least the shopping mall on a Sunday! Victoria Wood may have been being funny when she said church was what we did before garden centres, but the laughter has a hollow ring. Parents who are both working long hours during the week and whose children are with carers during that time, may well feel that Sunday is a time for family building, or just doing nothing. Then there are the people whose lifestyle choices make them, rightly or wrongly, feel that church would not be for them anyway. People who have survived without church for ten or fifteen years are going to need a particularly strong reason to feel the need for it again – nothing less than radical conversion will do it. But people who made some sort of commitment in childhood and then drifted away for years are more likely to be inoculated against Christianity than to see it as a new and radical way of living.

Also the way church operates is for many people – including our youngsters – a put-off. We live in a world of images and symbols. Even the news now comes in soundbites. Word-based messages are simply not going to be heard in our culture. Yet most church services are very word-based. How many of us of any age voluntarily sit and listen to one person talking for half an hour without stopping or being interrupted, anywhere apart from in church? How relevant is this format to the younger generation who even at school learn interactively?

There is also, and perennially, the clash of cultures. The young people are not like us; they don't understand our needs and we certainly don't see the need for their likes and dislikes. Take the vexed subject of music. While we like the traditional hymns or even the rapidly becoming traditional music of Graham Kendrick, the youngsters like something with no tune, lots of rhythm and maximum volume. We may feel that their songs have no content; they don't understand the words in ours. There are many other potential tension points. They may seem irreverent in their way of speaking to and about God. We can clash with them over what is appropriate clothing or behaviour, Young people like to feel approved of, as we all do, but often in church they find the one place where they are not allowed to be themselves.

There are other reasons why the teenagers are not staying in church. The teenage years are the time when idealism can spill over into intolerance. They see the faults in the church clearly, and decide to have nothing to do with it.

We seem to have taken the most relevant message in the world ever, and made it irrelevant, and even our own children are rejecting it, turning their backs on it, and voting with their feet. The church's mission is to bring the good news of Jesus to the world. The hard fact is that we are losing, or neglecting, the closest, most available and most open section of society – the next generation in our own families. If we can't convince *them*, how on earth are we going to convince anyone else? If those we live with reject our offer of life, what have we got to offer the world?

But are there mitigating circumstances? Is our task at the beginning of the twenty-first century significantly harder than at other times in history? It is a fact that there are factors in society that make the job of evangelising our children harder than in previous generations. (Though I have a feeling that every generation has looked at their world and decided that they have a harder job than those coming before!) Looking at society in the west we can see that there are many things outside the church that make it hard for our children to come to faith in God. In a pluralistic society, there seems no guarantee that ours is the true religion. What is truth anyway? If we can work out what it is, does it matter anyway? Is God in any sense relevant in the high-tech world into which our children are growing up? Consumerism and an ever-increasing affluence lead our children to think that what they can see and own is all there is. Individualism and 'me first' militates against Christianity. Our children are growing up into a world where the technology is changing daily – and they are keeping up with the change even if we cannot. The mobile phone is probably as necessary to today's teenager when getting dressed in the morning, as clean shoes were to some of us at their age!

The family is under pressure. Marriage is no longer the norm for our children's generation, nor is keeping sex for within marriage. Alternative 'families' are presented as equally valid alternatives; lesbian families, single parent by choice, living together, serial marriages and so on. The view of children outside the church varies from seeing them as a 'fashion accessory' to 'a right' to 'a mini adult'.

We are told our teenagers will rebel, but it's normal and necessary. We are told the experts know best. We are told the generation gap is unbridgeable, that teenagers and young people are a different species. The media tells them that about us too! We can look at all this, and assume that the slow trickling of haemorrhage, draining of our young people away from church is inevitable. But this state of affairs isn't inevitable; our God is the God of the impossible and we can change the environment not just for our own young people but also for their friends, if the church regains its purpose as salt and light in the world where it is.

Think for a moment about the society into which the church was born. In the first century the Middle East was in many ways remarkably similar to twenty-first century Britain. The expansion of the Roman Empire facilitated the spread of ideas, religions and trade from all over the known world. There was openness to new ideas and to travel that had never been seen in the same way before. There was also traditional Judaism, which gradually became more and more hostile to the growing church. Yet the church spread; persecution in Jerusalem just meant that the good news about Jesus scattered into many towns and villages, which would otherwise never have heard. There has never been an ideal society for the spread of the Gospel and there never will be. There is always going to be opposition; it is always going to be a fight. As Ron Kenolly says in one of his songs 'the battle goes on between the kingdom of darkness and the army of God and there *is* no demilitarised zone.' Jesus promised that he would build his church and the gates of hell would not prevail against it. The dictionary definition of 'prevail' is 'to be greater in strength or victory'. The gates of hell, with all the hosts of hell behind them, never ever had any chance of beating us; all they could hope to do was resist us, to keep us out. But Jesus promised they cannot even do that. They will have to fall before the church, which will then sweep in and claim hell's captives – our children among others. But only if we start fighting harder, and if we start using all the weapons he has given us – the greatest of which is our faith in him.

The army of Israel was scared. They knew God was on their side – in their heads! But in their hearts it was a different matter. Their eyes saw the armour and the weapons of the enemy. Their ears heard the mocking taunts of the enemy champion and when they looked they saw he was taller and wider and uglier and more muscular than any of them. So the knowledge of God being on their side, which was in their heads but had not been burnt into their hearts, was squeezed out by their fear. This was the army of Israel, the professional soldiers, this panic stricken rabble of boys in men's bodies. But along came a young musician. He wasn't trained to fight; he had come to court to entertain the king with his music. How much physical training and how many muscles do you need to play the harp? He knows he can beat this Philistine, but still the lies come, 'You are not able to go out against this Philistine and fight him; you are only a boy and he has been a fighting man from his youth.' What a good job David didn't listen to the lies. David relied on what he did have – creative faith and a small stone!

Centuries later Jerusalem lay in ruins and the people were scattered. Nehemiah and a few other returned exiles were working to rebuild the walls.

This time the lies and taunts came from the people of the area who didn't realise that God was involved in the rebuilding; 'What are they building – if even a fox climbed up on it, he would break down their walls of stones.'

But the walls were rebuilt and the city was inhabited again. The builders ignored the taunts and relied on what they had – determined faith and cooperation.

Throughout history God's people have been faced with lies, lacks and misunderstandings. We are no exception.

Society throws us lies about children.

Misunderstandings about the overwhelming love and grace of God and the relationship between obedience and blessing may affect our expectations of the way he works.

A clear vision of how God's love is extended to us and the implications for church and family life may be lacking. The result of all this has been that the children are ssssnot following us into faith. Nor are their friends. Nor are our neighbours. Nor is the world. God has not changed. He is still the God who went out with David and gave him the courage and conviction to use the weapon he was skilled with to bring about the defeat of the mighty Philistine army. God gives us weapons too, with which we can defeat the hosts of hell and keep our children safe in the Kingdom.

Part two

Keeping the body healthy

An examination of what the Bible has
to say about covenant, rebirth and
children.

Chapter Four

Understanding Covenant

God is a faithful God. Do we believe it? We sing it. We hang on to it when things go wrong. We stand inside our Christian ghetto, looking out at a world gone crazy, and whisper it to ourselves to hide our fear. But is it true? We dedicate our children to him as babies, or have them christened, then watch as they grow away from him. Is it true that he is a faithful God?

Of course it is. When a child dedicated to him as a baby, follows him faithfully throughout childhood, and then writes a letter to his parents apologising in advance for the fact that his A level results would in all likelihood turn out to be lower than predicted, 'because it's more important that I talk to my friends about Jesus', it's true. When those results turn out to be straight As, God is faithful. When a young lady who has struggled with dyslexia throughout school, decides at the age of twenty-three to go to Bible college to study for a degree so she can become a missionary to Native Americans – he is faithful. When a girl studying for A levels while ill with M.E. says, 'This illness has brought me closer to God – it's really a privilege' – it's true: God *is* faithful – though sometimes we only discover how faithful when we cry to him out of despair.

Yet for many families it seems that the evidence of this faithfulness is sadly lacking in our lives and the lives of our children. Is this because we often don't really believe it? We know it in our heads, but our hearts, our emotions, still think it will work for other people but not for us. Perhaps we don't know what God's faithfulness means in the pressure of daily life and how to rely on it and experience it in our own lives.

Sometimes, in exploring the meaning of a concept it is helpful to look the word up in a dictionary. The entry for 'faithful' reads; 'Adhering strictly to the person, cause or idea to which one is bound; worthy of trust or credence; consistently reliable'. There is an echo of this in the traditional words of the marriage service 'forsaking all other, be faithful to each other as long as you both shall live'. Faithfulness therefore means commitment throughout life. Since God lives forever, his commitment is eternal. But what is that eternal commitment to?

• *God is faithful to his creation*

He sustains it and without his active involvement nothing that we see could continue to exist. His commitment to this world is seen in his promise when Noah and his family left the ark. God promised never again to flood the earth.

> I have set my rainbow in the clouds and it will be
> the sign of the covenant between me and the

earth.... Never again will the waters become a flood to destroy all life. [Genesis 9:13,15]

• *He is faithful to individuals*

When he called Jeremiah, who thought he was too young and incoherent to serve God or carry his message, the Lord said,

> Do not say, I am only a child. You must go to everyone I send you to and say whatever I command you. Do not be afraid of them, for I am with you and will rescue you. [Jeremiah 1:7.8]

• *He is faithful to families*

His promise to Jacob when he was an old man was:

> Do not be afraid to go down to Egypt for I will make you into a great nation there. I will go down to Egypt with you and I will surely bring you back again. And Joseph's own hand will close your eyes. [Genesis 46:3.4]

But he is not just faithful to individuals or families.

He is also faithful to communities
To mankind as a whole.

> Abraham will surely become a great and powerful nation and all nations on earth will be blessed because of him. [Genesis 18:17]

Faithfulness can only be proved over time; by definition it needs time to be shown to exist. History is a demonstration of God's faithfulness. The Bible is the story of his commitment throughout the years, to the human race and to the task of reclaiming the world. In the beginning God created a perfect environment for mankind. When he had finished making the wonderful variety and richness of the world, he looked at it and pronounced it 'very good.' All the conditions were the best they could be. Humanity was not an experiment; God gave us the perfect ecosystem for our spiritual and physical well-being. But we doubted his love, and thought we knew better and so sin entered this perfect world. God's creation was spoilt, and mankind has through that sin at the beginning and through endless ages since, continued to hand over our inheritance to the forces of evil and rebellion. God did not, as we all did as children, screw up what he had made and throw it away to start again with something else. God is committed to his creation, and so he put into practice the rescue plan that had been in his mind since before time began.

The world God made, and gave us to live in is an understandable and reliable world. We know that day follows night, water freezes at zero degrees, and that apple trees will only produce apples, never strawberries. Natural laws of cause and effect are part of the creation God made, and we rely on them. Because humanity is designed to live in harmony with God and with each other, I believe laws of cause and effect operate as surely and inevitably in the spiritual realm as they do in the physical world. So, if we touch fire, we are scarred by burned flesh. If we hate our neighbour, our emotional health is damaged, and we can become bitter and twisted. If we choose to go against God, we will find sin and evil enter our lives as a result. The world we live in, with broken lives and fractured societies, is a result of choosing our own way over God's, time and time again throughout history, as individuals and as societies.

Yet throughout history God has been committed to repairing the damage. He chose a man, then a race, to be his people and to show the rest of the world the right way to live in God's world. The Old Testament is the story of God's covenant commitment to that race. However much they disobeyed him, he was committed to them. When the Israelites were wandering in the desert, they had in the pillar of cloud and fire a visible proof that he was with them. That pillar was a sign to them that God was with them. More than that, it was a sign that he was directing them, because,

> In all the travels of the Israelites, whenever the cloud lifted from above the tabernacle, they would set out, but if the cloud did not lift, they did not set out – until the day it lifted. [Exodus 40:36, 37]

God was actively and intimately involved in the ins and outs of their life, the ups and downs of the tent pegs, day after day. There was no way they could forget that they belonged to the God of Abraham, Isaac and Jacob. Even 'the stranger within your gates', simply by being there, belonged. When they arrived in the Promised Land, they knew they belonged exclusively to an exclusive God because all the people already in the land, worshipping other gods, had to be got rid of! They would often have wished that he would leave them alone to be like the other nations, and not to have to worry about this troublesome thing called holiness, but that was not part of the covenant – God was committed to them, and like it or not, they were his.

Even though God knew, before they even arrived in the land, that prosperity would have the effect of dragging them away from him, even though he warned them that this would happen, he still remained committed to them. Each time they turned away he sent prophets or teachers to lead them back to him. Even in exile, he did not leave them – their only hope of getting back to their own land was founded on the fact that they were the people of God. Throughout post-biblical history this knowledge that God was still committed to them is what has kept the Jewish nation going. They have an awareness of covenant in this global sense, encompassing everybody in the nation and going on forever.

God's endless commitment to humanity was given its ultimate test in the life and death of Jesus. God, seeing that men could never escape the dreadful results of sin on their own, fulfilled the demand for justice and punishment by taking it on himself. The death of Jesus – God Himself, is the final proof that God is committed, covenanted to his people. (It is also the final proof that Hell exists – if it didn't the death of God to save us from it was a mistake – a divine case of overkill. Sin and rebellion do have an inevitable and entirely just result – total separation from God.)

God, the God of justice and of grace, has been committed to humanity throughout all history. His commitment is to generations of real people, in real societal groups.

'Covenant' of course, is the legal and Biblical term for this kind of commitment – the commitment that God has to the world and its people. But covenant in its basic form is nothing other than eternal faithfulness. The Bible narrative is scattered with covenants; agreements between God and his people. We have already mentioned the covenant with Noah when God promised never again to flood the earth; however wrong things went in the future he would never again in this way destroy completely the living creatures he had made, either animal or human. In the covenant with Abraham, God promises to bless Abraham and make him a great nation and a blessing to all nations. As in all covenants the initiative comes from God. God spontaneously promised to bless and prosper Abraham. He didn't have to; he could have chosen someone else, or no one at all. But he chose to bless Abraham. This was God's side of the bargain; Abraham had only to believe him, and trust him. This trust would have its outworking in obedience; Abraham set out from the security of his ancestral home to a land that didn't even figure as a spot on his map yet, but was only located in the mind of God. This covenant was renewed to Moses along with the promise to bring them into the Promised Land. Again what God demanded from his people was obedience, and so he gave the law to Moses to help them understand what that obedience consisted of! Moving on through the Old Testament we come to David, to whom was given what is, not surprisingly, known as the Davidic covenant. God promised David that there would always be a descendent of his on the throne of Israel. Jesus is the ultimate fulfilment of that promise and the eternal outworking of it, because Jesus is forever the 'King on David's throne.' Jesus, being God, initiates and brings in the last Biblical covenant; 'the new covenant in my blood'. This time God is both the initiator and the sacrifice in the covenant agreement. He demands of us faith in the efficacy of that substitutionary death and ushers us into a new way of living based on grace not law. These various covenants are often given different names, but there is a real sense in which they are just different expressions of the same covenant.

'There is only one covenant in the Bible though it is expressed and elaborated in differing terms'. Each covenant promise is an evidence of 'the same amazing purpose of God to have a people for himself'. [J.A. Motyer *Introducing the Old Testament* Falcon Press 1963] Each covenant promise is initiated and confirmed by God; 'The entire initiative and the entire form of the covenant are within God's authority and not man's.' [ibid]

So we are a covenant people. William Dryness in *Themes in Old Testament Theology* [IVP 1979] lists these common characteristics of all the Biblical covenants:

1. They include a solemn promise.
2. They expand through history.
3. They evidence, on God's part, a desire for communion with a covenant people.
4. The relationship is not just of suzerain/vassal, but also of father/son.
5. The blessing of the covenant is dependent on obedience, though the basis of the covenant is not.
6. The requirement is 'a life of obedience in which his holy character is to be reflected'.

We also should notice that [5] above can be expressed in this way; 'The first word which God speaks to his people is a word of grace and only secondarily a word of requirement' [J.A. Motyer.

Op.cit.] This is important because it gives us a clue as to how we should live under this covenant but also how we should mediate the covenant to the disciples or learners among us. Grace must always come first; Jesus died before we deserved it. Love always has to give another chance. God is committed no matter what. But the proper response to the covenant promise is compliance to its terms. So obedience in life follows grace. Covenant living is the response to and result of covenant grace. Within the church acceptance always has to come first – for the children as well as for new converts or seekers. The model is 'I belong, therefore I believe' not 'I believe, therefore I belong'. Our children need to know that they belong now, whether they are five or fifteen. They need to feel that belonging brings acceptance and affirmation. They need to be able to live under covenant grace, God reaching out to them before they have any idea who he is, as he did to Abraham. Your church tradition may put a strong emphasis on the need for a significant day of conversion. I think mine (Baptist) does too. But for me it seems we have to accept the 'in but not yet fully of' that I am suggesting should be the norm. We are all on a journey closer to God; the important thing is the direction we are travelling. This will be dealt with in more detail later when we discuss the nature of faith. For the moment let us just note that this is a possible interpretation of Biblical material.

Throughout history God's covenants with his people have not been just with individuals but with the whole of the community – Abraham and his family, Moses and the children of Israel, David and the Jewish nation, Jesus, and the whole world. Though in each case God spoke with a single man, who was in some way representative of the nation, the blessing and responsibility were for all the people. In a similar way, on the cross, Jesus made a promise to the dying thief; 'Today you will be with me in paradise' which is the promise that he offers to each Christian since who trusts him and takes him at his word.

Awareness of covenant in this sense is something the church needs to reclaim. When we in the church talk about covenant it tends to be on an individual level – 'I commit myself to God and he will commit himself to me'. We don't see that this is actually backwards. God is already eternally committed to us and all we need to do is turn and acknowledge and accept that commitment. In the Methodist *covenant service* we find the words, 'give us grace to draw near with fullness of faith and join ourselves in a perpetual covenant with you.' While this is a perfectly valid response to God we need to remember that Biblical covenant is initiated by God, formulated by him and accepted by us. God is committed to us whether or not we respond. But the response is the means by which we begin to live in the good and the blessing of the terms of the covenant. This response is said by individuals but the covenant and the impetus for setting it into place is not ours but God's. It goes like this; 'I am your God. You are mine. Your family is mine. Your children are mine. Your community life is mine. Forever and ever. Amen'. That's what the Israelites got; that's what we've got, if only we realised it!

Just as the Old Testament covenants with Moses, David and Abraham looked forward into the future, so does Jesus' covenant with us. For God's covenant is not only for individuals, it is not only horizontally linear, it is multidimensional, comprehensive; it is not only for now, but also for the generations, not only for here, but also for everywhere. The Bible history of the Children of Israel is a demonstration of that covenant working out through the generations. This commitment that God demonstrates to his people throughout the generations is something we need to reclaim. God wants our children to love and serve him, they are his covenant people because we are, and he is committed to keeping them. God's covenants span space and time, including present day, past and future.

When I was a young Christian in the seventies, there was a phrase we heard quite often – 'God has no grandchildren'. Then, there was a tremendous, and important emphasis on the need for a personal response to God; we each needed to make an individual commitment. But in stressing the personal, we have lost sight of the community. The pendulum needs to swing back. It is obvious that a child brought up in a Christian home, prayed over from birth, and probably before, taught about God and shown Jesus in the way his parents treat him, is in a different position with regard to spiritual things from a child whose parents have no concept of, or relationship with, God to pass on to him. In this sense, God does indeed have grandchildren. The children of Christians are in a special relationship with regard to him. One parent expressed this as, 'At Christening we gave her back to God; she was always his.' This is not only a spiritual effect; it can be seen as belonging also in the realm of cause and effect that we live with day by day in all sorts of ways. We readily accept that children of dysfunctional parents are almost inevitably going to grow up with dysfunctional traits in their own lives, we know teenage mums breed teenage mums and that abusers are often the result of abuse in their own childhood, yet we are scared to claim that good also can be passed down. Yet the Bible confirms what we know in our hearts and see in society;

> Know therefore that the Lord your God is God; he
> is the faithful God keeping his covenant of love to
> a thousand generations of those who love him and
> keep his commandments. [Deuteronomy 7:9]

Evil is infectious but surely so is good. God promises to be faithful to the children of his servants. Our covenant relationship with him should extend to and be passed down to our children as Abraham passed it to his. Our obedience should have an effect on our children and their children's children. We should believe that they belong now as children of the covenant and will continue to belong as part of the future people of God. Their buying into the covenant will be much more likely if we think of them as part of it already. The ten year old daughter of a friend of mine said the other day, 'I don't think I will be able to find a Christian boyfriend. The only Christian boys in my school are my brothers. But I don't want to have a boyfriend who isn't part of us.' She already had a sense of being part of something special. I hope she does find a suitable Christian boyfriend, but I pray much more that she will never lose the sense of covenant that she is expressing, even if she doesn't yet know what the word means. We are the covenant people of God, from the oldest pensioner to the newest baby.

The beginning of John's Gospel is relevant here. John writes, 'He came to his own, but his own received him not'. This is presented at one level as a fact, but at the moral level there seems almost to be a sense of outrage in the mind of John as he writes - the Evangelist sees it as something monstrous: How could anyone reject such a wonderful destiny? Ownership on God's side confers 'right' on man's: 'to them he gave the right to become children of God'. God gives those who live in his community the right to become his children. In essence the Gospel transcends family and nationality, but nonetheless the idea seems to be that God 'owned' the Jewish nation who therefore had a right to be children of God. However, this right was not guaranteed but needed to be exercised through faith. Similarly, the children of Christians have a right to be told about their inheritance and therefore there is an obligation on parents and church to tell them, but in the end they have to accept or reject Jesus for themselves. But with the privilege of this right to be told the Good News comes a greater condemnation if they reject. Even Jesus had some hard words about the Jews of his day being more culpable than Sodom! So we have to make belonging so attractive, so compelling that they won't reject it, or him. They are, as children of Christians in a real sense, his own, and we don't want them to lose their place in his kingdom by rejecting his offer.

However we also need to admit at this point, because I want to write a book about the real world, not a fictitious one, that for some families and in some churches the reality has been that the children do not grow up into faith. Some children, and it almost seems particularly those of missionaries or pastors, turn their backs on God and cause great anguish, heart searching and maybe guilt in the parents. Sometimes we can say, 'if I'd done such and such, things would have turned out differently', but we cannot know that for sure. Jesus himself told us that families would be divided; ' a man against his father, a daughter against her mother.' [Matthew 10:25] It can seem that the love for God and sacrifice for him in our own life can be what turns the children away. Sometimes, it has to be said, it is. But equally it can be what inspires and challenges them to take on such a course for themselves. Ultimately everyone makes their own choice to follow or not, to run with the baton or let it drop. And even that is not our own choice – it is always and only the grace of God. 'For it is by grace you have been saved, through faith, and this not from yourselves, it is the gift of God –not by works, so that no-one can boast.' [Ephesians 2; 8] We can never guarantee salvation by what we do, either our own or that of our children, but we can, and must rely on his mercy and grace in their lives, whatever they make of him.

Belonging within the covenant of promise, as Paul expresses in Galatians, is because of faith in Jesus and what he has done, not in any works of our own. 'You are all sons of God through faith in Christ Jesus ... If you belong to Christ, then you are Abraham's seed and heirs according to the promise.' [Galatians 3:26, 29] Belonging comes because of faith, and faith comes by grace, as a gift from God, not as a result of works. It is true that we cannot force our children into the Kingdom, and sometimes despite all we do, they continue to reject the truth we believe in.

Sometimes all we can do is not enough, but we are only responsible for our children while they are children. As adults they are free before God to make their own choices and choose their own way. Sometimes, this will not be the way we have prayed for, but that doesn't mean we will stop praying or trusting God for their ultimate turning to him. And if changing the way we are as family, or as church, can reduce the numbers who are drifting away from faith, then those changes are worth making. Reclaiming the idea of covenant community is a first step that puts parents and churches in a proactive rather than reactive mode.

Chapter Five

Generational Promises

Have you ever noticed how many family trees there are in the Bible? They are the bits we skip over; not only do they appear boring, just a list of names, but most of those names are impossible to pronounce anyway. We are not likely to listen when (if) they are read in church, or to choose them for our Bible study passage. So the family trees, or genealogies tend to be ignored. But we know that they must be there for a reason; after all we know that 'all Scripture is God breathed and is useful for teaching, rebuking, correcting and training in righteousness.' [2 Timothy 3:16.]

So what does God want us to learn from these genealogies? Probably several things, but with regard to what we are thinking about, if nothing else these genealogies show us that God is involved in, and cares about the generations. God loves families. God saves families. Not just in lateral relationship – brothers and sisters – but in temporal relationship – children's children. The Bible tells us that God's covenant is wide, but also long. God promises to bless the descendants of those who love him for a thousand generations!

His commitment to humanity is specific. He doesn't just 'love people'; he loves us as individuals but in context. So God loves people within their families and races. He sees generations as important. Family line and ancestors matter. God commits himself to his people in time and in space. The nation of Israel, his chosen people, began as a single man and his immediate family, and grew to clans and tribes. Notice how God spoke to Abraham; 'I will make you (singular) into a great nation and I will bless you.' [Genesis 12:2] In obedience to God's command Abraham then sets off with his family. 'He took his wife Sarai, his nephew Lot... and the people they had acquired in Haran.' [Genesis 12:5]

The nation of Israel developed from this – a nation made up originally of one family, all with some of the same genes. God's first call and promise to Abraham stretched down the centuries. God committed himself to Abraham's family, and to the generations of families that succeeded him, becoming as they grew, the nation of Israel. Then he began to call himself, 'The Lord, the God of your fathers – the God of Abraham, the God of Isaac and the God of Jacob' [Exodus 4:15]. God was the family's God.

The Biblical family is nothing like our Western fictitious-ideal nuclear family. A biblical family was in some ways a much more untidy entity, consisting of parents, grandparents, aunts, uncles, cousins, children, servants and 'the stranger within your gates.' As the Israelites travelled through the wilderness the community was made up of tribes, which in turn were made up of families like this, and groups of families, all sharing in a combined life experience.

Family is fundamental to community. You cannot have community without families. Families, by definition, span the generations; we look back in time to our own parents and grandparents and forward in time to our children and their children whether born or unborn yet. By anchoring ourselves in this chain of people we know who we are. Similarly, God looked at Abraham's small family and saw in it the future – a whole nation of families worshipping and obeying him and blessed by his presence and protection. God is himself family; three persons in one, communicating, relating, loving, working, with a shared purpose and power. This is his ideal for families generation after generation. God is a generational God.

From this nation Jesus was born. God's physical involvement in humanity is within a specific family line, hence Jesus' genealogies in the Gospels. We know who Jesus is, humanly speaking. We can trace his ancestors back on his father Joseph's side all the way to Abraham, passing on the way David, thus fulfilling the promise God made to him. We know that his mother was related to Elizabeth, the wife of the priest Zechariah. God himself became part of a family with ancestors who could be named, and, through his brothers and sisters, probably descendants carrying the family line on. We had an interesting conversation the other day about how everyone must be related to Jesus, through his relatives who have kept the genetic line going. Whether or not there is any truth in it, it is an interesting theory, and it does show how clearly Jesus is anchored within a recognisable genealogical line and how committed God is to mankind.

This emphasis on God being involved with families is traceable throughout the Bible, though with less emphasis after the life of Jesus. How often in the Old Testament God is referred to as, 'the Lord, the God of your fathers'; for example in Judges 2; 12. . It is almost as though God is basing his right to be recognised and worshipped on the fact that the forefathers recognised and worshipped him. In a strange mutual sense, God belongs to the generations of his worshippers, as they belong to him. Jesus himself makes reference to this timeless, or time transcending aspect of covenant when he rebukes the Sadducees in Matthew 22; 31-32. They are questioning him as to whether there is such a thing as resurrection. Jesus quotes Exodus 3; 6, ' I am the God of your father, the God of Abraham, and the God of Isaac and the God of Jacob', in order to show them that they are wrong. God is still God of the past generations. He is God of the present and he is God of the generations still to come. That is covenant – generational covenant. It is right, and natural and to be expected, that we will worship our father's God, and that the following generations will worship ours. He is committed to our family line, as he was to Abraham's and we should be committed down the family line and into the future, to him.

In Psalms we read ' This God is our God for ever and ever.' [48:14] This is primarily a statement of truth and but it is also a statement of faith. This faith is something we, at the beginning of the new century seem to be losing sight of. We look at the numbers of young people leaving the church and we see a dark future when he is no longer our God. Our fear in the face of trends dwindles our faith away. Yet the reality is that God delights to save families, down through the future for ever and ever, as the Psalmist knew. He is love; the family is a demonstration of his love and a growing place for love of each other and of him. He loves our children, and their children. He loves the idea of generation after generation faithful to him, because he is faithfulness personified, and he is faithful to them.

God covenants with families. Throughout the Old Testament his promises are ' to you and your children'. We have already seen this in the covenant promises to Abraham [Genesis 18-19] and David [1 Chronicles 17] for example, but there are other instances of this wording. In their response the people's promises to him also include the children: 'As for me and my household, we will serve the Lord.' [Joshua 24:15] This seems to be not so much specific children or even specific generations but more of a promise and intent to, as a family, be faithful to God for ever. This is echoed in the New Testament; Paul tells the jailor; 'Believe in the Lord Jesus Christ, and you will be saved – you and your household.' [Acts 16:31]. Just as God's commitment to us is eternal and unchanging, so is ours to him, and as parents we have the right and the duty to make that promise on behalf of our ungrown children, and to do all we can to make them take it on for themselves as they grow up. It is our responsibility to do everything we can to hand the baton on. If the kids drop it, that is their responsibility. But if we let it hang limply by our sides, we are at fault. They cannot drop what they are not handed!

However, if we are faithfully trying to hand that baton on, we have plentiful reason for believing that it will not be dropped. God promises over and over again that the children of those who honour him will be saved. Talking about the righteous man, Psalm 25:1 says, 'his descendants will inherit the land.' Inheriting the land was a sign in Old Testament times of acceptance into the nation, the people of God. The land was God's and his people lived there. Only those who were part of the covenant community had the right to inherit the land. Again, in Psalm 102; 28 we read, 'The children of your servants will live in your presence; their descendants will be established before you.' Think about what established means; made stable, made secure. Something that is established is not easily moved. What a comforting thought that our children can live, secure and established in God's presence.

We saw in the chapter on covenant that covenant consists of both promise and require-ment. Obedience is what is required on our part and God gives the blessing. But if we decide to ignore or neglect the covenant it is negated by our action, even though God is still holding the promise out ready for when we come to our senses and once again fulfil his demands on our life. It is the children of the Lord's servants who will inherit the land and be established. In the New Covenant brought in by Jesus 'obedience is effected by the placing of the law within the heart and by the work of the Holy Spirit'. [Paul Witcher] *The Significance of the Abrahamic Covenant in the Old and New Testaments* 1993 unpublished) So these promises about the children, of which there are very many and of which I have only picked out a selection seem to be formulated in a covenantal style; this is the blessing, this is the responsibility. If we are not seeing our children blessed, then it seems we have only our lack of obedience to blame. Sometimes, of course, disobedience is the result of ignorance, but to quote a phrase often used in a legal sense, 'ignorance is no excuse.' The promises are there for us to read:

> Blessed is the man who fears the Lord; his children will be mighty in the land; each generation of the upright will be blessed. [Psalm 112:12]

These promises are not in the Bible to mock us; what God promises is always achievable. We take the promise of new life literally. We believe Jesus means what he says when he promises the Holy Spirit. Why should we not believe that God says exactly what he means when he promises that our children will be mighty and blessed? There is nothing more straightforward than this verse – if we take his promises to Abraham and Moses and David literally, then surely we have to take these more general promises literally.

> I will pour out my Spirit on your offspring and my blessing on your descendants. They will spring up like grass in a meadow, like poplar trees by flowing streams. [Isaiah 44:3]

Both grass and poplar trees are naturally 'planted'; they do not take great effort, or treatment of soil, or special climatic conditions. Grass will colonize any bare land, and all a poplar tree needs to flourish is damp roots! It is natural that Christian, God honouring parents should see their children become Christian, God-honouring people too.

> All your sons will be taught by the Lord, and great
> will be your children's peace. [Isaiah 54:13]

This is part of Isaiah's prophecy about the future glory of Zion, according to the heading in my Bible but surely it is also a promise of the blessings brought in by the coming of the Kingdom of God, here and now in our lives.

> And I make a covenant with you; I have given you
> my power and my teachings to be yours for ever,
> and from now on you are to obey me and teach
> your children and your descendants to obey me for
> all time to come. [Isaiah 59,21]

This verse was written in my Bible when my first child was born and has been a special promise for our family, ever since. Twenty three years on, both our children are stronger and more mature Christians than their father and I were at their age.

But how can we believe these promises if we never hear them? When the voices in our ears from the media tell us our children are lost to us almost before they are born? Because these promises are the *truth* –they are in the Word of God and there are too many of them to ignore. But we have spiritualised them, or seen them as belonging to then and not to now, or just not known they were there. This generational aspect of faith needs to be taught in our churches and talked about and prayed into being. God is concerned about the next generation.

If you have never read, or never appropriated God's covenant, generational promises; if you are afraid for the future of your children, get a marker pen and start reading them! God is more committed to your children's salvation than you are. If they are dedicated to him, he has a very real vested interest in making sure that they become part of his Kingdom. This is a truth that flows throughout the Bible, but which to a large extent we in the Western church have lost sight of, because we have been so influenced, even blinded, by the lies and myths we have been fed about our children, They are part of God's Kingdom, and belong to him. He is committed to them, if we are his people.

All this means that there is a very strong bias towards the continuation and transmission of faith down from generation to generation. God's 'passive' intent is that it will happen this way. In a sense, as well as natural laws of cause and effect, which we take for granted – plants die without water, drinking too much alcohol causes pain- God's spiritual universe has 'natural' laws of cause and effect and the blessing of faithful children is the inevitable result of a life of faithfulness to God. As a flower naturally grows towards the light, so the children of Christian parents naturally tend towards God. But when we focus our eyes on the problems, the dangers, our own fears, instead of his covenantal promises, we are in some way preventing the promises being fulfilled. A climbing plant may need a trellis to allow it to grow up towards the light. Take away its support and it may just tangle its way along the ground. Our faith in the generational promises of God may be the trellis our children need.

In education there is the concept of the self-fulfilling prophecy. It has been proved that children learn better if you tell them they are clever and praise every little thing they get right. But if you then treat those children with less care, criticize them and do them down, their rate of learning slows down. Surely this idea, the self-fulfilling prophecy, can apply in other ways too. If we think our children will turn away from God, we are preparing them, and ourselves for it to happen. But if we fix our eyes on his promises and intent for them, we are preparing ourselves for this to happen and allowing it to be so in their lives.

But because God is a covenant making God his promises cannot be one sided. Their fulfilment is dependent on our response. He will always be faithful, but we must be faithful too. And the flip side of blessing is cursing, of promise is warning. God's favour rests on those who obey him, but his disfavour must be expressed towards wilful disobedience. This too we find in his word.

> He will turn the hearts of the fathers to their children, and the hearts of the children to their fathers; or else I will come and strike the land with a curse. [Malachi 4:6]

Can we not see that this is true; we do live in a cursed land because fathers and children are not united in love of each other and of God?

God's covenant promises call for a response – obedience! There are by definition two sides to a covenant. The conquering King sets out his conditions and rewards, and the defeated king promises obedience and submission. There are many and very clear commands about our children and how we should bring them up. Introducing them to Jesus, teaching them the basics of the faith, seeing them grow up strong and faithful, is our duty and our privilege. The Bible tells us to 'bring themup in the training and instruction of the Lord' Eph 6:4. It is not optional; it is not something we can leave to the Sunday school teachers, to the experts or to chance. It demands that we look at our own relationship to God. The promises are for the righteous man, for the one who obeys. It has rightly been said that blessing is not a result of belief, but of obedience. The righteous man, whose life is lived in close fellowship with God, is blessed by the same privilege being bestowed on his children. Our obedience and devotion to him results in a similar lifestyle for our children. But this is serious stuff; the children are our responsibility and we need to be aware that God holds us responsible for correct teaching and training. What we do in this area affects our own relationship with God. While I was studying for this topic, this verse jumped out at me. Jeremiah 1; 6. 'Why should I forgive you? Your children have forsaken me and sworn by gods that are not gods.'

Isn't that a chilling word from God! It seems that he will hold us responsible if our children do not follow us into faith. I did not want to write this because it seems so hard – but it is the truth. We are responsible for transmitting the truth and the reality of our faith to the next generation. But we need to do it together – church, community, family – in whatever form allows most freely for God's promises to come true. Let's take God at his word – he loves our children; he is committed to generation after generation serving him.

Chapter Six

Regeneration – Trauma or Growth?

Did you know that, according to Christian Research's findings, 80% of people in church leadership today made a strong commitment to God in their childhood? The mission societies are full of people who were 'called' as children. The youth work associated with the church would probably fold completely if it were not for enthusiastic and mature young adults who met God and committed themselves to him in their childhood. This interesting fact cannot be just coincidence. Why is it that most people in 'authority' within the Christian church and parachurch organisations are those who became Christians at an early age?

We live in a world that runs on laws. One is that the more you practice something, generally the better you become at it. Practice makes perfect – and this applies as much to faith as it does to everything else. The goal of our Christian life is that we become more like Jesus. He is the only perfect human but he is the measure of what we have the potential to become given that God is at work in us. The Bible tells us that God's purpose is to have many sons just like Jesus. 'Those God foreknew he also predestined to be conformed to the likeness of his Son, that he might be the firstborn among many brothers.' [Romans 8:29] As children of God we are supposed to grow more and more to be like him. None of us become Christians and are immediately perfect in character and knowledge. Maturity takes time, whether we are talking about apples or faith. The Holy Spirit works in us to develop Christ-likeness over time. People who have a real encounter with God in their childhood have a definite time advantage in growing to spiritual maturity. Obviously I am not claiming that people converted later cannot become mature Christians, and must remain all their lives spiritual babies, but young people who are really committed to God bring their youthful enthusiasm and ability for learning and trying new things to their faith. Even among 'ordinary' Christians 70% make a commitment before the age of twenty. Dr Peter Brierley in his document 'Leaders' briefings 13' containing the results and implications of his research for the Christian Research Organisation found that the average age for making a commitment to Christ was likely to remain under 20 for many years to come. He concludes that it is therefore vital that we reach these young people. I would add that it is particularly important that we do not lose the ones who are already 'christianised.' There is an optimum time for making life decisions, and it is while we are young.

Our worldview inevitably affects the choices we make about life goals and occupations. So people who have made a strong and life affecting decision for God in their teens or earlier, will be taking this into account when they make decisions about education and career choices. A commitment to follow God may well influence university course choices, or even whether or not to go to university. The desire to share in God's mission to the world may lead to working in the church or in mission organisations either short or long term. I know of various committed teenagers who had worked with gypsies in Albania, led a team working with street children in Brazil, run a children's holiday club in Southern England, learnt to brick lay in Tanzania, done street evangelism in Zagreb, met with teenagers from all over the world at a youth conference in Germany, or taken part in a mission to Manchester which involved renovating run down areas of the city – all before they were nineteen. Their summer holidays from school or college were filled with exciting and challenging activities, which developed their maturity and stretched their faith. All this early experience contributes to leadership qualities in later life. For those who make a decision for Christ in their early years it opens their eyes to a world in need and a world of opportunity at a time when they are free and enthusiastic enough to be changed by it and idealistic enough to believe that they can change it! Working for and with God at a young age also means that their faith is tested and therefore strengthened. They will be helped to know what and why they believe.

In the society into which our young people are growing up, whether they are heading to further education or out into the world of work, their faith will inevitably be challenged intellectually, and the Christian lifestyle ridiculed. The children who keep their faith and weather the storms of our humanistic education system and the rocks of university with its freedoms and adventures, are those whose faith is real and personalised, not just habit handed down by their parents, or worse, a compulsion put on them from outside that they cannot wait to break free of. The young people who keep their faith in their workplace are the ones who have made it real and valuable in their own lives. We need to help the next generation to grow up into faith, not away from it. They are capable of real strong faith well before they reach their late teens. If, as is the case, church leaders mainly come from people who became Christians in childhood, for the health of the church as much as for their own sakes, we need to do all we can to help our children into faith.

So we can all agree that for a child to come to faith is a good thing to happen – good for the child and good for the church. But what does coming to faith mean? What sort of faith can a child have? How does the change that we call new birth happen? Jesus said, 'Unless a man is born of water and the Spirit, he cannot enter the kingdom of God' [John 3:5] But he also said, 'Unless you change and become like little children, you will never enter the kingdom of heaven.' [Matthew 18:3] Do you think these two statements are contradictory? Can a small child be born of the Spirit? Do we need a conscious day when we can say, 'Before this I was not a Christian, now I am'? Over the years opinion has been divided, and swung backwards and forwards as to whether a child is 'in till it opts out' or 'out till it opts in.'

Depending on our churchmanship we will be likely to hold one or other of these views. Catholics in general, with their greater emphasis on community and belonging seem to hold to the former, while evangelicals, with an emphasis on personal response seem to move towards the latter. But there is a third possibility, which is 'growing gradually closer until he is definitely in.' Richard Hubbard, a children's evangelist, puts it this way;

> At one time I was always keen to know exactly how a person had become a Christian, and, more importantly, when! … Now I understand much more that God draws people over a period of time and he sees their hearts and understands where they really are with him.
> [*Taking Children Seriously,* page 32]

The Report from the General Synod Board of Education published in 1988 as *Children in the Way*, a deliberately ambiguous title, states

> For a long time our understanding of individuals growing in the Church has largely been in terms of intellectual development rather than faith development.

But belief in Jesus cannot be an intellectual development – otherwise our degree of salvation would depend on our IQ! I am fully saved but you cannot be because you do not understand it all! This is patently nonsense.

John Westerhoff in *Will our Children have Faith?* expresses the growth of faith like this;

> A tree in its first year is a complete and whole tree, and a tree with three rings is not a better tree but only an expanded tree. In a similar way, one style of faith is not a better or greater faith than another.

He goes on to describe a four-part development of faith – from experienced faith, to affiliative, to searching, to owned. Experienced faith is what we all start with, where or faith is dependent on what we do and feel. So a child brought up in a loving warm home, will understand God to be loving and warm like that because that is what life tells him. Later we need to feel part of the 'community of faith' and story, communal worship and acceptance are important. At this stage affiliative faith is a shared faith; doing things together becomes important. Within a family situation, a child will believe itself a Christian because the significant adults in its life are. Searching faith internalises all this and looks for faith and faith responses within oneself rather than experiencing them through the worshipping community. If our children are going through this stage they need to be able to talk about it with all sorts of different people. Their views may change from day to day, and we need to ensure we provide lots of useful and faith building input in their lives. This it not the time to back off and allow them to struggle through on their own. Though it has to be said that for some children, as they grow up, they want to worship in a different church or with a different style of worship.

At this stage we see the importance of Christian friends as well as of other relevant caring adults as a child grows into independence and their own chosen style of worship. This will lead them towards the final stage – owned faith, which is to know who we are and what we believe. This brings the ability to stand up for what we believe even against peer or community pressure. This model can be helpful in our thinking not just of children coming to faith but also how we need to treat those outside the church in order to help them grow into faith. Westerhoff says that this pattern allows for slow gentle growth in faith as well as the day of conversion model. It is important that we do not read into the searching stage the necessity for rebellion. I do not think that rebellion in adolescence is either necessary or to be desired, which it would have to be if searching faith always implied it. Searching, and coming to faith does not have to be a process of rebellion and returning, as we shall see if we look at one of the stories that Jesus told. It has been said that there is a 'God shaped hole' in each of us, and that only when we find God is that hole filled. But this need not even be a time of searching; it may be just a recognition that 'it fits'.

You remember the story that we now call the prodigal son? There was a farmer- not a 21st century British farmer for this one was rich! This man had two sons. The older, a quiet hardworking lad helped his father on the farm, doing anything he was asked. The younger, in the way of younger sons, saw that he couldn't match up to his older brother's example, and predictably, decided two people working was plenty, and he was going to have some fun. He bullied his father into giving him his inheritance, and set off for the bright lights of the city. There, he found how popular money could make him, but also how money vanishes unless wisely invested. He spent the next few months feeling very sorry for himself, feeding pigs. Remember, this was a Jewish lad; to him pigs were not only muddily unclean, but also ritually unclean. However many times he washed out the pigsty, they were still revolting to him. Yet, he was so hungry, he even pinched the bread crusts, and squashed overripe fruit, before he tipped the rest of his master's household waste into their trough. So he too became muddily and ritually unclean. At last he came to his senses and trudged back home, intending to improve his situation by asking permission to care for his own father's sheep – neither so muddy nor so taboo! But the father had spent night after night not sleeping, praying that his son would get in touch, that somehow he would know this boy was all right, and day after day scanning the horizon in the hopes that his son would see sense and come home. When he saw that dejected, dirty figure on the road the father dropped everything and ran to hug his son, filthy and smelly as he was. Imagine the party – the returned son washed and cleaned up, dressed again in the smart yet serviceable clothes he'd once despised, eating the good food, feeling happy to be home at last, realising as never before, how much his father loved him.

Why did Jesus tell it? The answer is obvious; it was to show that God's forgiveness is endless, and that he rejoices over the repentant sinner. That he cannot wait to welcome us into the fullness of our inheritance in him. That's all. Really? Indeed, that is enough. As a picture of God the Father, waiting, longing for us to return to him, it is wonderful. Jesus couldn't have given a more compelling picture of God's infinite willingness to forgive. And for those whose children have grown up away from faith it is in this respect a great encouragement. The son remembered the good things he had known and leant from his childhood, and it was that memory that drew him back. Similarly for our children, some, who insist on rebelling, will be drawn back by the memory of true and good things in their past.

But Jesus tells this parable to show us how very much God loves the repentant sinner, not as an example of how to become a Christian. It is a picture of the heartbroken and yearning love of God. It is encouragement that however far from the Father we have strayed, he is always waiting to welcome us back. It is descriptive, not prescriptive; we are not all meant to go off and have a fling with sin and the world before we come to God. It is a graphic and easily understandable illustration of God's love – a love which always waits, and hopes, and welcomes, and cleans, and restores. It is *not* a parable illustrating that via rebellion is the only way to come to God.

If it was, I don't believe there would be an older son in the story. This purpose would have been served just as well if Jesus had made the prodigal an only child. But there is another child. Why did Jesus include him? What did Jesus mean us to learn from his picture of this rather resentful older brother? I think it is because there is another truth that he wants us to see. We need to know that regeneration does not have to be trauma; it can be growth.

No father would prefer his child to behave like the younger son in the story; neither does God. Ask any parent who has lost a child to drugs for years – they would much rather have a stay at home child, even if he was sulky occasionally. So, I believe, would God. There are many ways of coming to

God. The Bible tells us that 'all have sinned and fall short of the glory of God.' None of us is completely free from the smell of the farmyard. Even the stay at home, hardworking older brother often smelt of the livestock – and sheep can be very smelly too! The Father values and cares about those who grow up with him, learning gently to love him and trust and serve him while still rejoicing over those who go wildly astray and then return. There is great love and understanding in the father's words to his older son, 'My son, you are always with me and everything I have is yours.' This son had faithfully obeyed and loved the father throughout his youth, and the relationship between them is one of companionship and shared work. In a very real way, this older son was growing up into his inheritance. But sadly, though he spends all his time with the father, and does whatever he is asked; though he knows himself loved and valued by the father, he still does not understand the love of the Father for the lost and the silly and the destitute. Living with the Father, he doesn't realise how great the Father's love is for him either. He can't see that all the things his brother gets are his anyway, just for the asking. He doesn't realise that the steady relationship he has with his Father is worth more than all the feasting and presents. But the important thing about him is that the relationship is there. I think Jesus included this rather ungracious older brother to show that this too is a way to relate to God – growing up in his family. Rebellion is not to be desired, it is not even necessary, despite what the psychologists tell us – children who grow up into faith, knowing themselves loved by God from birth, may, like this son, have gaps in their under-standing to be sorted out, but they are blessed by an ongoing relationship with the father, growing up into a mature relationship with him. The younger son would always have the memory of his foolishness and the wastefulness of his time in the big city. He would never forget how much he had let his father down. The older son knew unbroken fellowship with his Dad, and even the rebuke given in this story, is only cause for a moment's reflection. Must'nt it be much more blessed to have grown up from birth knowing Jesus, secure in the love of a heavenly Father, as well as earthly parents, and to have unbroken love and fellowship with him, than to have to go through trauma and evil before realising his love.

How does all this apply to our church leaders from the head of this chapter, and the lost children that we are considering throughout this book? If we believe regeneration is trauma, and the prodigal son is the normative pattern, then we are far more likely to allow our teenagers to rebel, to accept their leaving the church and to tend to delay any serious teaching or spiritual demands on them. We will not try so hard to keep them. We will accept wilderness years. If however we believe that new birth can be a gradual process, which I believe is true and which I think this parable also shows, we will be looking for and expecting God to work in and through our children. Even if we accept that there are 'stages' of faith which they have to work through, we can see that these can be extended or shrunk according to God's purposes and dealings with the child. A child who has its own unique personal experience of the living God will no more be able to deny God's existence than he will his own. Children who have real unique and personal experiences of God in their own lives, will as stated elsewhere find it very 'difficult to turn and walk away'.

How many of our children really meet God and see him working? If he is real in their lives as children he will be real as they grow up. But where are they going to meet him? It needs to be both at home and at church. They need the experience of worshipping in a live and relevant way, and seeing their parents' generation being worshippers, but they also need to see the Christian life lived out day to day at home. Jesus at twelve was discussing with the finest minds in Jerusalem. This was not a result of years spent colouring pictures in Sunday School, but years learning what the Old Testament says, and applying it. Obviously, it can be argued that Jesus was a special case, but he was also a fully human child, and our children are made in his image. Our children need to see the reality of God for themselves – in inspiring and challenging worship, in practical living, and in their own homes. Unless Jesus is a real person and part of the family, he is not going to be real to them. Unless they are a real part of the church they are not going to feel any sense of belonging to the people of God.

We need to be aware that we are in a battle. Satan has never stopped trying to get control of this world. His biggest triumph is when he succeeds in spoiling what God has created, particularly if that is the life of a human being. The battle is for the souls of our children and the state of the church. Remember the statistic about church leaders mentioned earlier. 80% of them made a solid commitment to Jesus in their childhood. Think what this means. They grew up into faith, tried and tested that faith in their teenage years, and having had childhood to mature in, were ready and willing for God to use them as young adults. The Jewish Bar Mitzvah ceremony is a sign that this is the way it should be; the ceremony celebrates the arrival into the community of Israel of a child grown up physically and spiritually. We have a responsibility from God and to our children to raise up the next generation of warriors for him. We have a responsibility and a trust to send them out into the adult world as ready and equipped as we possibly can, so that they are strong and useable for him. Not least because the battle is hotting up – the world they grow up into is more alien to his rule than it ever has been. We want them to grow peacefully into their inheritance as children of the Father. We must ensure that we send our children out into their world ready, equipped, wise and strong. If we do not we are letting them down and we are letting God down.

Chapter Seven

God and Children

It was dark in the Temple; only the flickering light from the golden lamp stand pierced the darkness and shone on the outspread wings of the golden cherubim placed at either end of the sacred ark. Eli, the priest, had retired to his bed, but little Samuel, the Temple servant, lay down in the temple itself, covering himself with a thin blanket. The golden cherubim didn't frighten him; he had known them since he was very small. The fading light from the oil lamps was comforting and warm and soon he slept.

Suddenly he sat up – Eli had called him. He ran on bare feet over the cold floor. 'No I didn't call you, go back to sleep,' Eli said sleepily. Poor Samuel, he'd no sooner got settled than the voice came again, and again he ran to Eli. Same response. By now, of course, Samuel was wide-awake, and was lying wrapped in his blanket when the voice came a third time. Samuel sat up. He was puzzled now, because he wasn't sure it sounded like Eli. But then, who else could it be? Again he trotted over to Eli's bed, and Eli this time was wide-awake enough to realise that it must be God. He told Samuel how to answer and sent him back to bed. So Samuel lay down again. Would God really speak to him? Surely it was Eli that God would choose, not little Samuel. But sure enough, the voice came again, and Samuel answered.

We don't know whether Samuel slept again after this; the Bible just tells us that he 'lay down until morning.' How reluctantly he must have opened the doors to the Temple, not wanting to face Eli, not wanting to pass on the message he had been given in the middle of the night.

How old was Samuel when all this happened? We don't really have any clues, but I don't think he could have been very old because he was sleeping in the Temple. He was still a child, and remember that for Jewish boys childhood ended at twelve.

Children are important to God. Though they are little in size, and possibly wisdom, he has special purposes for children. Samuel is an example of a child who was chosen and used by God even from birth. At the time of this story, Israel was in a bad way. In some ways Eli had been a good and honest servant of God, but he was not the world's most successful father. He had failed to teach his sons any respect for God and the rituals of his worship in the Tabernacle. The sons discovered a good way of getting a good meal without having to cook or pay for it; they extorted the best pieces of the sacrifice that the Israelites brought, by demanding it as the priest's portion. They also took advantage of their position to sleep with the serving women. Eli's way of dealing with this was a rebuke, which was ignored. He had left it too late to discipline his sons, and the respect for God and his ways which he should have taught these two young men throughout their childhood, was missing. Notice that God blames Eli – it is his fault for not bringing them up properly, allowing them to disobey the laws that he and God demanded of others.

> Why do you scorn my sacrifice and offering that I prescribed for my dwelling? Why do you honour your sons more than me…Those who honour me I will honour and those who despise me will be disdained. [1Samuel 3:29, 30]

The effect of Eli allowing his sons to behave in this way was that God's promise was taken away. Both Eli and his sons paid the price of disobedience. It is fashionable to claim that we have no influence on how our children behave- it's not our fault if they turn against God. But God sees it differently – we *are* responsible and will be required to answer for the behaviour of our children. This may be an area where the church as a whole could need to repent. When our actions, in church or at home, have driven our children away from God, when we have not done all we can to build in them respect for God and his ways, when we have not prayed and modelled and taught, that is sin. Sin needs to be repented of. God holds us responsible for what we make of our children.

To return to Samuel; though a small child, he was given a very serious message from God when Eli, by ignoring his sons' evil behaviour, had to some extent closed himself off from God. God told him that the punishment, which he had previously warned of, would indeed take place. Eli had obviously been more successful in teaching Samuel to love and honour God, than he had been with his own sons. Maybe he had learned by his mistakes. Samuel grew up to have a very special relationship with the God who first spoke to him when he was a small child. But his ministry began when he was still the Temple servant. He seems to be a demonstration of the principle we saw in the previous chapter – calm and gentle growing into faith is possible.

God was also with David in a special way during his childhood. When did David begin to compose the Psalms? Was it when he was alone with God and the sheep? He need not have been more than eight or nine – on a recent holiday in Morocco we saw children of that age caring for flocks on their own. David must have spent a lot of time in God's presence to have such a wide and deep knowledge of who, and what, God is. Imagine young David, the smallest of the family, setting out with his flute or a little harp, to watch the sheep. He saw the beauty of what God had made, in the hills and the countryside, the flowers and the rivers. He heard the birds, listened to the wind. He remembered the stories he was told week by week about what God had done, and he listened to God himself in those long solitary days. His love for and confidence in God is evident in the book of psalms, where so many of us still go for comfort, for inspiration and for praise. Not that he wrote all his songs when he was young, but the time spent alone in the hills with his God must surely be reflected in the words he used to worship. His childhood experiences of God's protection and enabling were also what allowed him to face bravely the huge Philistine champion who struck fear into the hearts of Israel's soldiers. He knew that God was with him because God had also been with him when he had had to defend his sheep from the lion and the bear. Childish faith, perhaps, but true faith, when he declares to Saul,

> The Lord who delivered me from the paw of the
> lion and the paw of the bear will deliver me from
> the hand of this Philistine. [1 Samuel 17:37]

God then vindicated that faith, as he does time and time again when his young servants put their lives on the line for him.

In case you think that these are special famous people, and therefore different, what about the little girl we read of in Judges 11? Her father Jephthah was 'a mighty warrior'. Setting off for a battle with the Ammonites he made what seems in hindsight an extremely foolish vow to God. In return for victory, he would sacrifice as a burnt offering the first living thing that came out of his house to greet him on his return home. What did he imagine it would be – his dog? A slave? Before we even read on in the chapter, we know that this has the potential for tragedy. Sure enough, having heard of the victory, and watching eagerly for her beloved father to return, out came his daughter dancing and playing her tambourine. This is one of the stories we really wish was not in the Bible. How could God let that happen? But it is, and he did and which of them was firmer about the necessity to keep your promises to God? The little girl of maybe 12 years old! She must have known God for herself to even contemplate what she said. She knew you take him seriously. She knew, didn't she, that to die with God is better than to live without him!

God does put his hand on children from birth. He does speak to very young children in very clear and direct ways. This is not always easy for the child or for the parents; sometimes God's dealing with his little ones seems far harsher than we would like, or even want for ourselves. But ask a child who knows the reality of being called and used by God and they would not have it any other way. I saw my son called to evangelism at the age of twelve; not a nice peaceful call for sometime in the future, when he was big enough, but a day and a night of anguish when God convicted him with tears of his lack of concern for the souls of his friends now. As the Bible says, 'It is a terrible thing to fall into the hands of the Living God.' But it is also a wonderful thing; those whom God calls, he loves, he cares for, he strengthens, he guides. The ideal for a child is to say, as David says, in one of those Psalms we mentioned earlier,

> You brought me out of the womb; you made me trust in you even at my mother's breast. From birth I was cast on you; from my mother's womb, you have been my God. [Psalm 22.9]

We underestimate both our God and our children if we think that they have to wait until they are older before he will use them. We impoverish both the child and the church if we don't do everything in our power to enable them to be used by him. I am convinced that for a child, just as for an adult, the only safe place to be is in the centre of God's will, but that that centre is a very much bigger and more exciting place than the whole world outside it. Childhood is not always a comfortable place for anyone, but children who see God working and participate in what he is doing, are growing in ways that their 'pagan' peers know nothing about. Maybe part of our difficulty is that we in the west have intellectualised our faith – we think being a Christian is knowing *what* we believe whereas really it's knowing *who* we believe. The acquiring of knowledge does need maturity but the building of a relationship just needs love. The smallest child is capable of love and of knowing itself loved. God is able to be the real and full Saviour of the smallest child. Even a baby can respond in love to him. It is nonsense to say that they are not capable of faith until they are old enough to understand. If that is the case, I am not capable of faith either, because I cannot understand why God should ever love me or how he could possibly die for me. Yet, I know he loves me, and through Jesus I can respond to that love. What more does anyone need to know?

The Bible tells us that children are a gift from God; 'Sons are a heritage from the Lord, children a reward from him.' [Psalm 127:3]. God's gifts are always good, but to a certain extent what we do with them is up to us. It is within our power to neglect or misuse them. If we continue to do that, then eventually we lose them. The gift of children is no different from any other, except, sadly, in this case, if we do, it is the gift that suffers, as well as the recipient. With the change in attitudes towards children, and the greater ability to plan and limit family size according to human wishes, isn't this what has happened in our western societies today? Children today may not be seen as gifts; we don't see how precious and special they are to God and we forget what a tremendous responsibility and privilege he has given us in our children. We have frightening power over the children when they are small. It is within our ability to damage them irreparably. The way we treat them affects their whole life. The schools we choose, the activities we encourage, the friends we allow, the church environment we expose them to, all have long-term effects on them. The best thing we can do for them is to introduce them as early as we possibly can to the God who knows them best and will never make mistakes in his handling of them.

Have you ever thought of the significance of the way Jesus – God incarnate – came into the world? This is an impressive way in which Christianity shows itself both more amazing and also more plausible than any other 'god becoming man' story. Jesus, by being born a baby, and growing through all the stages of childhood in a normal and natural way, showed that childhood is a valuable and unmissable part of being human. God identified totally with his creation, by living as a human being from conception to death, just as the rest of us do. So God understands children from the inside, not just because he created them, but also because he was one. Imagine for a moment, what it might have been like. He had a 'normal' childhood, experiencing the things that children throughout the world have experienced both before and since.

Think of him as a baby born, like many others then and since, in poverty and squalor. Then as a refugee, traveling through the night into a foreign land, to escape the cruelty of a frightened, despotic king. Then later, imagine him as an excited toddler, coming back to his native land, for the first time hearing everyone talking in the language his parents used. Imagine his little hand on the saw, with Joseph guiding it, as he cut his first piece of wood. Imagine big brother Jesus, admiring each new baby as it joined the family, later making up wonderful games for his younger brothers and sisters, sorting out their squabbles, telling them stories. Listen to Joseph and Mary praying with him, teaching him about his Heavenly Father, telling him again the events surrounding his birth. Look at Jesus among the other boys in the synagogue school, drinking in the truth about his Father and his dealings with his people, memorizing the words of the prophecies which, even then, *did* he realize were talking about him? Even more mind boggling – think of Jesus as a teenager, growing lanky and ungainly, then with the first fuzz of a beard appearing. Think of how his relationship with his parents changed over those growing years, as maybe he took on gradually more and more work in the carpenter's shop. Did he make window frames and tables for the houses of Nazareth? We are given no clues in the Bible, apart from the story of the visit to Jerusalem when he got left behind in the Temple, about his childhood, though there have been imaginary 'gospels' written which claim amazing miracles for him even as a child. (One such is the Gospel of Thomas for example which reads like a modern horror story, having Jesus making live birds out of clay at the age of five, and killing a playmate who upset him. It is so far fetched as to be laughable) So I think we can safely assume that there was nothing very supernatural about Jesus as a child, but that he was 'super' natural – the model of what childhood is and what growing up should be and was designed to be. Better, but not different from our children. I think this is significant because Jesus, the perfect man, was also Jesus the perfect child. You cannot imagine him rebelling as a teenager. So the experts who tell us teenage rebellion is necessary and to be expected are talking absolute rubbish. This is a point that I keep coming back to; I think it is important because it has been the reason for many teenagers getting out of church and into trouble. It is perfectly possible to grow up into adulthood without the trauma of broken family relationships. The generation gap does not have to open up.

Jesus knows about children because he was one, and unlike many of us, I don't believe he forgot what it was like. So Jesus knows exactly what each child needs and how each child is capable of responding to him, at any stage in their development. If we are open to it, his Spirit can feed into their lives at any stage whatever it is that they need to know. So my three year old, suffering from severe eczema, at bedtime one night said with complete conviction, and longing, 'In heaven, my skin won't itch.' And went to sleep peacefully, leaving his mother in tears, hoping it wouldn't be that long before the eczema went. (It wasn't!)

But when he grew up, did Jesus ignore the children and concentrate on the adults. This would seem the sensible way of going about things – after all, adults can think clearly, they have the power and the influence, they have useful connections. But no, the Gospels are full of children. Jesus healed them – Jairus' daughter, the Syrophenician woman's daughter, the widow's son, the boy with the evil spirit. He healed adults too of course, but he seems particularly moved to compassion by children. He also allowed children to help him; where would the five thousand have been without one little boy's lunchbox? He enjoyed their praise; they sang as he entered Jerusalem, and their praise was special to him, so important, that if they were forced to stop, he said, the stones at their feet would take up the music. He valued their love; children knew Jesus would welcome them, even if his grumpy friends wanted them to go away.

Now let's look at some of the passages that show Jesus dealing with children to see if they give us some clues as to how we should treat them. Our first is a very familiar passage. [Luke 18:15-17]. Here is Jesus telling parables to the crowds. They see this as very important business – even though he is really just telling stories! So when the women come with their children, the disciples rebuke them, telling them to go away and not bother the teacher, or sharply saying, 'Don't interrupt.' Jesus however blesses the children, and then turns them into a visual aid for a very important message. On a first reading, we assume that these children were maybe four of five and Jesus was telling us to be like them in their spontaneity, openness or trust. In fact these particular children are likely to have been much younger, no more than babes in arms. It was the custom for mothers to bring their children to the rabbi on their first birthday for a blessing. This is probably what these mothers were doing. So, if the children were only a year old, what Jesus is commending can only be their complete dependence. Is he telling us that we can only enter his kingdom if we come in *complete* dependence? Are we to understand that the key to the kingdom is love – not knowledge or understanding?

In another passage, [Matthew 18:1-3], Jesus calls a child to stand among them. This child is older but not much as it is still described as 'a little child'. So here, Jesus could be commending humility and obedience. However, I believe this is to miss the whole force of this passage. What Jesus is telling us here is that our right of entry to his kingdom depends on our response to children. 'Whoever welcomes a little child like this in my name welcomes me. But if anyone causes one of these little ones who believe in me to sin, it would be better for him to have a large millstone hung around his neck and to be drowned in the depths of the sea.' He repeats it later, 'See that you do not look down on one of these little ones.'[Matthew 18:10] Can this be right? Yes, because it ties in with the rest of his teaching, and indeed the thrust of the Old Testament; we, as God's representatives are to care for the sick, the poor, the dispossessed, the powerless. All of which can apply to children. Although children today in the west appear to have more rights, freedom and power than ever before, is not our society dispossessing them of the one thing they need more than anything else, the right to a life lived in the way God intended? By not teaching and not modeling the life of Jesus for them, we are causing them to sin. Jesus said, 'little ones who believe in me.' Modern child psychologists have 'discovered' that small children have an innate sense of the numinous or the presence of the spiritual dimension in the world, which they tend to lose as we put them through the education system. Modern life teaches them not to believe. Small children do have faith, and we need to nurture and protect it, not destroy it.

To sum up, Jesus knew children from his own experience of childhood and family life, he knew the Old Testament inside out, and knew God's angle on children in it, he also has a truly unique insight into the make up and psychology of children because he created that makeup and psychology. If ever children felt loved, affirmed and rightly valued by an adult, it was when they were with Jesus. The experience of those lucky few in first century Israel is one we want to replicate for our children today – not just that they are introduced to Jesus, but that we in our dealings with them, model his way of treating them.

Part three

Blood transfusion

Ways of bringing health and vigour
back into the church community.

Chapter Eight

Living inside the Covenant

So where have we got to? We've seen that everywhere church congregations are shrinking, and this shrinkage is predicted to continue, as the smaller number of young adult and teenagers move away from faith into an adulthood where church does not figure at all and so a whole generation of unchurched children will grow up. The draining away of the younger end of the church has been likened to a haemorrhage. The blood is going out and with it life and vitality. The church is literally dying of old age.

There may be many reasons why this state of affairs has come about. However looking back and wringing our hands or apportioning blame is neither necessary nor constructive. Church and family together must work to stop the haemorrhage. The nuclear family and the faith family all have a role to play, but we can make a difference and so to speak put a tourniquet on to prevent more loss. It is in the family that faith should be caught and taught – not primarily in the church building. The people who are responsible for teaching and training are the parents. But church structures and leaders have a vital role in equipping and supporting parents in their very difficult task.

So how does the concept of living within God's covenant affect our family and indeed church life? If we are covenant people, subject to, yet lovingly cared for by the provisions of a far higher power, what difference does this make in practical terms?

Covenant means security

We live in tremendous security. If as church and as family we know and claim God's covenant promises, we find that the responsibility for our continued existence is not ours, but his. As we have seen, the Bible is full of promises for the children of God's people. We need to know what he said so that we can claim it. If you are left a fortune in the will of a distant relative, you cannot claim it until you are aware that it exists. That is what solicitors are for! In the same way, if we don't know what God has promised, we won't expect it and we won't know what to ask for.

As we all know, and can probably remember learning the hard way in childhood, promises are no good at all without the will and the power to make them come true. God's power has not changed. At any time and in any place throughout the universe, he is in control and will fulfil his word. Yet we can still be tempted to look at the world outside and see our family as a frail insignificant organism that inevitably will be swallowed up by the predators outside. We are not frail weak organisms; we are God's blueprint for community living. God invented family and he has a vested interest in seeing it survive. He can and does fulfil his promises. He did it for my family and my church and he will do it for you. He delights to save families and he wants your kids in the Kingdom too, far more than you do. I believe he has great purposes for the present young generation. Children and young people who have had no church background at all are coming to faith and they will need strong, mature young people to train and disciple them. They need united families to be a demonstration of what family can be, to give them role models where their own may be non-existent. They need young enthusiastic leaders who are now equipped to lead and teach and serve, precisely because they have spent their childhood learning the basics.

Living within the covenant gives us greater security and knowledge that the future is possible, and full of hope.

Covenant means provision

Another aspect of God's covenant is that our resources and provisions are also his responsibility. Our response to the things he gives is grateful acceptance. Yet in a rapidly changing technological age, we can be left so amazed at what man has achieved that any idea of God's power remains far from our thoughts. The 'fear of the Lord', so popular a phrase in centuries gone by, is now an almost unknown emotion. Fear of course, has many different meanings, and these days in this phrase would be more likely expressed as 'awe'. We would not want to fear God. We would acknowledge our awe and amazement at who he is. This is a healthy emotion. The fear of the Lord is an inward sense of his holiness, his otherness and yet his immanence. It means zealousness for his honour. It is the emotion that caused Jesus to clear the moneychangers out of the Temple – because they were misrepresenting God and what he stood for. He was totally unafraid of the priests, the Romans, the Jewish people, everyone, because he was so wrapped up in God and reverence for him and his house. In our families and our churches do we talk about God and wonder at what he has done? It is evident that we in the West hear and talk a lot about what mankind has done, and rightly so. As I write this I am using wonderful man-made technology, which allows me to change spellings and delete patches of print only to have them reappear elsewhere. In the kitchen I can hear the washing machine doing all the scrubbing and rubbing my grandmother used to do by hand. When I have finished this chapter, I will send a quick email to my daughter in America – halfway round the world in seconds. Outside, my car waits to speed me to places that are too far to walk. When I open the newspaper I read that genetic engineering of plant material will solve the world food shortages and that the human genome is being mapped. There is so much man-made splendour that gets in the way of what God has done.

But God also deserves credit for what he has done. For man fails dismally at genuine fundamental creativity. Who made the genome that we are so proud of mapping? Who makes the plants grow that man alters genetically? Who put the metal ores deep into the ground for us to find and turn into useful metal for cars and washing machines? We cannot make a single really new thing. We cannot create; we can only adapt and use what has been created. In the moral realm too, we fail to be at all creative – having rejected God's order for moral values, mankind flounders around, trying and failing to find something equally valid to put in its place. Man neither has nor will ever acquire the abililty to create life out of nothing, as God did. Man can design beautiful gardens, but God created from nothing the beautiful mountain scenery we admire from afar. Even the inventions of technology, of which we are so proud, are only possible because God first provided the resources, both material and mental. Let's celebrate God's involvement in his world, in our church lives and in our family lives. Let's give the glory back to God, feel again a sense of awe at the world we live in. We should wonder at creation, beauty and moral goodness. Can we relearn and therefore appreciate the vast difference there is between God's achievements and mankind's? If the children grow up with this atmosphere, it will become natural for them too and gradually they will begin to regard God as a supremely powerful and awe-inspiring part of their lives. 'Awesome' is a word the youngsters use a lot –let's teach them who and what is really awesome! Awareness of being within the covenant encourages this sense of awe and wonder at the greatness of God.

Covenant means freedom from fear

Another thing that covenant living can free us from is fear. The Bible tells us that 'perfect love drives out fear'. [1 John 4: 18] Yet it is a fact that we do fear things, particularly things we don't understand. There are many adults these days who are afraid of children. They are so different from us. They are so at ease in the world of cyberspace. They are loud, confident, and even speak a language we don't understand. While we may not think we are intimidated, fear can affect our dealing with them even without us being aware of it. Are we afraid to lay down and enforce rules for our teenagers in case they shout, rebel or run away? Do we pacify and bribe our toddlers when we should be disciplining them? Do we allow our children to dictate to us, refusing to eat certain foods, to come to church, or behave when they are there, to do their homework? Are we afraid that our children will do something terrible and let us down in front of the church? Do we let them 'get away with murder' as a result? Interestingly, one of the factors that seems to be significant for young people who continued in faith throughout their teenage years was the expectation and even compulsion that they would go to church. Whether this is to the same church as their parents, or as sometimes happens choosing another, more 'youth friendly' congregation, the expectation by relevant adults that church attendance will continue is one way of preventing lack of faith. The very point that parents are afraid to insist on because of modern 'wisdom' can later become something that children looking back are glad happened!

Having spoken to many Christian parents, it seems that for many there is a mainly unspoken, but nonetheless real, fear that the children will turn out wrong and that there is nothing we can do to prevent it. This is simply not true; it is a lie of the devil. God made families to be a place of freedom from fear. He puts parents in control of their children and gives us responsibility to bring them up his way. God is not a cruel tyrant. He doesn't give us children, either in our families or in our churches, to show we can't cope; he gives us children to add to our joy and our responsibilities. We can rely on his perfect love for us and for our children. When we acknowledge our fears to him he can turn them into trust.

Covenant means holiness

The covenant terms always demanded total dedication of the people to the conquering ruler – from henceforth they belonged to him. In terms of our relationship to God this dedication is expressed in our willingness and ability to live holy lives. Holy means 'set apart' or 'dedicated'. As church and as kingdom people we are called to personal holiness. The Bible calls us a 'chosen people, a royal priesthood, a holy nation'. [1 Peter 2: 9] As part of God's Kingdom, we are meant to be different from those around us. Society around us calls seductively for self-fulfilment, self-indulgence, happiness. God calls us to purity, selflessness, sacrifice, unconditional love – and joy and peace. In the West, we have so much of the world's goods in material terms, we can begin to think like the world – 'It's my right', 'I need …', 'it's justified because …' But God says, 'Be holy, because I am holy.'[Leviticus 11: 44] Jesus commands, 'Be perfect, as your heavenly Father is perfect' [Matthew 5: 48]. A holy disciplined life brings glory to God and peace and satisfaction to the person living it. A holy, set apart, disciplined family is a strong witness. Family members who think first about each other's needs are showing God's love. God's people need to have open, transparent consistent lives, lived openly with each other and before God. There is a beauty in such lives as will draw our children to Jesus even despite themselves. There is a distinctiveness about families united in love and service to God that serves as a witness, a judgement and a challenge to those who have not followed his ways. It comes as a result of a desire for personal holiness, to be set apart as individuals and as a family for the service of a holy God. 'You will see again the distinction between the righteous and the wicked, between those who serve God and those who do not.' [Malachi 3: 18]

[Psalm 54: 18] 'All your sons will be taught by the Lord and great will be your children's peace.' God promises those who honour him that the blessings will continue to the children and the children's children. But he warns strongly that the responsibility for ensuring that blessing is appropriated rests with the parents. And there is a price to disobedience 'Why should I forgive you? Your children have forsaken me and sworn by gods that are not gods.' [Jeremiah 1: 6]

Covenant means true worship

Another aspect of the covenant God made with the Israelites was that he expected sincere, regular and relevant worship. He also expected it to be enthusiastic and understandable. A friend of mine is a worker in one of the Church of England dioceses. At the moment she is in the process of discussion and revisions of what goes on in the churches in her diocese. The Church of England is aware that its forms and times of worship are not meeting the needs or concerns of today's society. There is a perceived need for change. If we are honest, most of us will have had the experience of church seeming totally unrelated to our daily life. This is even more frequent for our young people. Church doesn't 'scratch where they itch'! Our times of coming together in worship are meant to bless God and inspire and equip us for living a committed life the rest of the time. We need to consider what sort of church structure achieves this. Much of what happens in church is based on a worldview that is sadly out of date. Our teenagers are not used to listening to words for any length of time –even their school textbooks are colourful and interactive. They are more interested in how they feel than in what they know, in what works than what is the truth. Church has variously been accused of being out of touch, 'Macdonaldised', modern in a post-modern society and so on. Sunday church meetings might indeed be all these things. But church is much greater than what goes on on Sunday; it is the people of God living and relating together. We have to find ways of doing this, and worshipping as well, that are relevant to the whole community, believers, seekers, children, young people and older ones.

Covenant means radical commitment

Paul and Silas arrived in Thessalonica. They had not been there very long when they were hauled up before the authorities. The charges were that they had 'caused trouble all over the world' or, as it reads in older translations 'turned the world upside down' [Acts 17: 6] Whatever else the citizens and officials of the towns of Asia Minor and Eastern Europe were able to ignore at this time, one thing they could never be in any doubt about was the fact that Christians had arrived in town! When the Christians arrived, the status quo was no longer static! Demonised people were set free, sick people healed, enemies reconciled, churches started, accepted standards challenged, magistrates upset. As if that wasn't enough, when the first exciting events had calmed down and life was beginning to return to normal there was a growing church of believers in Jesus showing his new way of living to a waiting world.

There are places in the world today where Christianity is 'turning the world upside down'. In parts of Central Asia, whole villages are being changed as Jesus comes in. In one place I heard of, a group of Christians entered the village in order to do some praying and teaching. The mayor of the village drove them out, saying they were not welcome. But later she begged them to come back – as a result of their prayers, people in her village had been healed of longstanding illnesses and she was convinced that Jesus was more powerful than her old religion. Not long ago I attended a church service in Almaty, Kazakhstan, where 61 people were baptised. Commenting on the large number of converts brought the response, 'That's nothing, last month it was over 100!' The followers of Jesus are still turning the world upside down.

But here in the West it isn't like that. Here, we are virtually indistinguishable from the people around us. The church in England has become conformed to the world to a greater extent than we are prepared to admit. The pervading materialism of the western world is just as alive and well in the church as outside it. Our children hear us talk about giving everything to God and see us clinging to our comfort and possessions. We have forgotten that God is a miracle working God and rely on the modern wonders of science, medicine and education! We have a false view of our relationship to God, confining it to two worship services on Sunday and a couple of midweek meetings. We have a false view of our relationship to his people, confining that too, to a nod and a chat on Sunday over coffee, and a meeting where we would never admit that things are not all sweetness and light. We have a faulty understanding of what God's Word really says, because we tend to spiritualise it and apply it to relationships within the church congregation, not seeing that it applies to family life and our relationships with the neighbours and their children. And our children, who have grown up in a world which taught them to see reality as fragmented and incomplete, don't know that we are short changing them. We confine our religion to church services, and they think that's the way it should be. So they have two standards, one for Sunday and one for the rest of the week. We think that's terrible, but don't see that they learned it from us!

There is a terrible lack in the church in western society; we have lost our total commitment to living God's way no matter what. We are like the rich young ruler. [Mark10: 17-22] He came to Jesus and asked what he needed to do to inherit eternal life. In the pride of his wealth, his breeding, his social position, he knelt in front of Jesus and asked for salvation on his own terms. We have no reason to believe he wasn't sincere. But the cost was too high. He could not bear to let go of the things that he owned, not realising that by holding onto them so tightly he was allowing them to own him.

We are so like him, scared to change and clinging desperately to our worldly security. We sincerely want to follow Jesus but like this young man, we ask again how much it will cost us. Some don't realise it will cost exactly what it cost Jesus – everything. Others realise this but turn their backs and twist his words, claiming that he didn't really mean what he said; he exaggerated to make a point – he couldn't really have meant that the nice sincere young ruler needed to give everything away, could he? The path of least resistance is to turn away and refuse that choice, to sell out to 'respectable' Christianity. Clinging to our security, lifestyle and privacy, we do not even notice that we too have missed God's best. Those who follow Jesus have rights to nothing but we make excuses and pretend that we are doing what he asks of us.

Following this encounter with the young ruler, the disciples pointed out to Jesus that they had left all that they loved to follow him, and he promised them more people to love and care about as a result, but also promised them persecution. We must be so determined to do what Jesus wants that it must be as if we hate these things compared with him;

> If anyone comes to me and does not hate his father and mother, his wife and his children, his brothers and sisters – yes, even his own life, he cannot be my disciple. And anyone who does not carry his cross and follow me cannot be my disciple. [Luke 14: 26-27]

As the rich young ruler found, if possessions or lifestyle are in the way, they must go, otherwise we risk losing out on salvation. We only want to give Jesus what we are comfortable with – he wants the lot! Nothing is guaranteed – only if we truly follow him, persecution. This sense of turning the world upside down is not how we would describe our lives; more that we are turning the church upside down to fit into the world. Or we are just marginalizing our religious life to such an extent that it has no effect at all on how we live our day to day lives.

Tom Sine in his book *Mustard Seed Versus McWorld*, puts it this way:

> What we have done, I am convinced, is to succumb inadvertently to a dualistic model of discipleship and stewardship. In spite of all the talk about 'Lordship', everyone knows that the modern culture come first. Everyone knows getting ahead in the job comes first. Getting ahead in the suburbs comes first. Getting the children off to their activities comes first. And we tend to make decisions in these areas pretty much like everyone else – based on our incomes, our professions and our social status.

When we have made these decisions, then we 'sanctify it' by looking around for a church where we can feel called to worship. To quote Tom Sine again;

> The problem with this dualistic model is that we not only sanction giving our first allegiance to decisions about where to work, live and entertain our young, we permit modern culture, as part of the deal, to define our notions of the good life and better future. As a consequence our lives are too often driven by the same manic aspirations that propel McWorld. No wonder we are exhausted. Modernity calls the tune and we dance.

There are very few Christians who actually choose primarily where they will live according to what God wants, unless they are out 'on the mission field' (abroad and probably in a third world country!). Normally the decision of location is mediated first by job prospects and only then by 'where the Lord wants us'. But the results when this order is turned round can be amazing. In the summer of 2001, *The Weekend Telegraph* Property Section had a feature entitled, 'Could these people raise your house price?' It was an article by Christopher Middleton about people belonging to The Message, which, as the article says. 'sounds like a cult but is, in fact, affiliated to the established church.' These young professional families have turned their backs on the normal climb up the property ladder and committed themselves to living and working in the rundown estates of Salford and Wythenshawe, Manchester. The reason they are there is 'as missionaries whose goal is to shine the light of God into the lives and back alleys of the community'. The interesting thing about this article, apart of course from the fact that it is reported in a way that shows the Christians in a sympathetic and positive light, is that the writer sees the possibility of their presence there actually improving the quality and resaleability of property in the area, and thus having an upward influence on house prices.

But how many of us have never even realised that this is the sort of choice we might be called to make? Jesus said, 'Whoever finds his life will lose it, and whoever loses his life for my sake will find it.' [Matthew 10: 39] And again, 'a man's life does not consist in the abundance of his possessions.'

[Luke 12: 15] We know these verses; we've listened to them in sermons, and nodded wisely; we've agreed with the sentiment; we've wished other people would hear them. But we have not heard them ourselves. The words go in one ear and out the other and never engage with our hearts or our lives.

I think that this gradual secularising of our lives is another reason why we are losing our teenagers and young people. One of the reasons given for leaving the church in *Gone but not Forgotten* by Richter and Francis is that they see the church as 'not having any immediate impact for good in the world' and not being 'the loving community they seek'. It is simply not true that young people do not like having demands made on them. We cannot use the demands that the church puts on them as an excuse for their leaving. We are not putting demands on them; we are busy showing them how we can escape the demands of Jesus' call for radical discipleship. But young people actually want something they can believe in passionately. They want to be challenged and involved and drawn by something that gives meaning and excitement to their lives. However,

> A major cause of decline is the sheer mediocrity and dullness of the religious life of the mainstream. Frankly it is boring. It opens no windows in the soul.' [Rev Kenneth Leech *The Sky is Red* Darton, Longman and Todd 1998]

The new generation need 'windows in the soul' opened; they need a church that is so demanding and enthralling that life without it would be unthinkable. Young people are looking for something that will inspire them, that will demand of them all that they can give and that will provide purpose and meaning to their lives. But the church in the West is not providing that something. If we are honest, it is not providing it for those of us who have not left either.

> This gnawing sense that the Gospel somehow does not apply to significant areas of our lives is one symptom of the sacred/secular divide that many church leaders regard as the greatest challenge facing the contemporary church. Of course we all believe that Christ should be Lord in every area of our lives but fewer of us feel equipped to live out that belief. [LICC programme 2000-2001]

The church needs to change; we need to 'discover how God is calling us to put God's mission purposes first'. [Tom Sine, *Op. cit.*] It must have been exciting to be with Paul and Silas as they travelled from city to city. There were sea journeys, there were confrontations, there were changed lives, there was fervent prayer, there were miracles. We may not be able to provide the sea journeys but shouldn't the church be providing this kind of pioneering environment for our young people. For unless the church is so radically different that what it presents is not just an 'alternative lifestyle' but a completely new way of interacting with the society in which we find ourselves which cannot be ignored, but somehow draws and compels, we will never be effective. Understanding that we are a covenant people, living in the security and blessing of that covenant, frees us to dare to live in this radical, world challenging way.

Whether we express it in terms of living within the covenant, as I have done, or in some other terms, it is important that we, both in church life and in home life, live out the reality of what faith in God is. The children need to see that it is real because, if we don't teach them, no one will. They won't get a real vibrant living relationship with Jesus from anywhere else. They won't get it from the schools, from the television, on the Internet, from their friends. Or at least, some might, but to risk leaving it to chance is stupid. The culture we live in is anti Christ. C.S. Lewis said,

> There is no neutral ground in the universe: every square inch, every split second, is claimed by God and counterclaimed by Satan.

Our church life and our home life really do matter and can make a significant difference in this cosmic battle.

The young people, our children, really are on the front line and they need all the help they can get. We need to take God at his word, claim them for him and him for them, and work with him to make his promises come true and bring our children triumphantly into the Kingdom. We should do all we can to make our homes places where growing up into Jesus is as natural and inevitable as puberty! We must proclaim the truth that God is a covenant, generational God. His love for families is wide and long. He is more committed to our children than we are. 'This God will be our God for ever and ever,' all down the generations – grandparents, parents, children, grandchildren – the people of God.

The one thing that you could say about Jesus was that he was not ignorable. He challenged; he threatened; he attracted; he repelled. But he didn't bore. Neither should his followers and neither should his church.

Salvation is not just an intellectual assent to a set of facts; it is a lifestyle lived in communion with a real, active, personal God, a God who talks. If the church does not speak into the world our children are growing up into, it does not speak relevantly and may as well be silent. As always our lives speak louder than our words. Can we find a way of being church that takes account of all we have seen and enables our children to grow naturally and smoothly into adult faith? If we save the world and lose our own children we have lost our inheritance, we have failed to claim and own his promises and we have failed to build the church as strongly as it might have been built. If we save the world, and lose our own children, we have failed. But if we save the children and ignore the world we have failed too. But failure is not in God's plan and he has given us the resources, the will and the desire to do both; to save outwards and to save downwards. Let's believe that we can, that he will, and start seeing wonderful things happening to and through our children.

Chapter Nine

What the Children Need

This book is not setting out to be another of those 'how to be a perfect Christian family' type offerings that tell you how to organise your family life so that it is crisis free and Spirit filled. The reason for this is that there are as many different ways of being family as there are families to be. What worked for us will not necessarily work for you. What I am hoping to achieve is to show that the loss of our young people is a church and family problem and needs to be tackled on both fronts. The way we treat our children in both a church and a home context, will inevitably have an effect on how they grow into and through their teenage years. So we are going to look at just the basic fundamental needs of children and see how we apply this in a way that remains faithful to what we know of God and is also relevant and, most importantly, achievable in the society in which we find ourselves. My premise is that if we learnt to be church, in an integral seven days a week wherever we are format, in the way Jesus intended, we would lose less of our young people and be more attractive to those outside the church.

God is a trinity; Father, Son and Holy Spirit. He created mankind a trinity too – body, soul and spirit. These three parts make up our common humanity and give us the unique attribute of being made in the image of God. We all have basic universal needs reflecting the complexity of our make up. On the physical level we need light, warmth and food. On the intellectual level we need stimulation, occupation and the chance to learn. On the emotional level we need love and companionship. To become full and mature human beings we need all three parts of our being to be fulfilled.

We are only just beginning to realise the long term effects on children brought up during their early years in the harsh and neglectful environment of an Eastern European orphanage, for example. It was thought that if they were brought out and put into loving families, their development would become 'normal'. But this has not proved to be the case – such children continue to have difficulties in making relationships and conforming to civilised norms of behaviour long after they are taken away from their orphanages. The optimum time for learning to form relationships was spent tied in a cot for twenty-four hours of every day, and something has been lost forever. This is not to say that we should allow them to stay there – it is an argument for even earlier intervention and also training and adequate staffing of such institutions to give the children the maximum possible loving and tactile contact and so to minimise the damage as much as possible. But it does provide us with a clear warning as we consider what children need if they are to grow up fully rounded adults, with a capacity to love people and to love God.

When their emotional, physical and intellectual needs are met, children grow with a sense of security and self worth. And this is what we want to give our children; security in our love, but much more in the love of their heavenly Father and a true sense of self worth based on the value that God puts on them.

Think about yourself. What makes you feel secure, loved or valued? Isn't it being with people who love you and understand you, who take time to be with you and care enough to be open with you? If you have people who will celebrate your successes, sympathise with your failure, correct your faults and stick by you anyway, you know that you have a value to them. This applies to children too; if we want them to grow up knowing themselves loved and valued, then we have to show them that they are. It has been said that home is where people are valued and values are learnt. This is obviously going to take time and effort. We will need to communicate values to our children. We will need to love them and we will need to discipline them. Children therefore can be said to have a trinity of needs – for communication, for love and for discipline.

The Bible gives clear guidelines about bringing up children. The problem is that they are scattered among other things and are not labelled 'childcare'. It would be so much easier if there were a book with that title somewhere between Corinthians and Galatians. But the Bible does not compartmentalise life in this way. Our childcare will depend on our lifestyle. Our lifestyle depends on a whole lot of variables. But one factor should remain constant; our commitment to God should affect every aspect of our life and that will inevitably include how we bring up our children. To the God who became man everything is relevant and everything is holy. The most important part of a person's Christian service may be bringing up the children into faith. Imagine what would have happened in church history if the Wesley parents had ignored their responsibility to their children and their God.

When God was giving his rules for living to his people in the desert, they were directed at a community, of which the children were an important present part and a vital future resource. They were after all, apart from Caleb and Joshua, the only people who actually entered the Promised Land. If they had not been well taught they might never have made it in or may have ended up being absorbed by the surrounding tribes. As the Israelites arrived on the banks of the Jordan, Moses expanded for them, the commands that had been given forty years before in the desert. Now the implications are spelt out for them and applied to the people who will settle in the land across the Jordan.

> These are the commands, decrees and laws the Lord your God directed me to teach you to observe in the land that you are crossing the Jordan to possess. So that you, your children and their children after them may fear the Lord as long as you live by keeping all his decrees and commands that I give you and so that you may enjoy long life. Hear, O Israel and be careful to obey so that it may

> go well with you and that you may increase greatly
> in a land flowing with milk and honey, just as the
> Lord, the God of your fathers, promised you.
> [Deuteronomy 6:1-3].

Notice that it is obedience that brings the blessing and the blessing is poured out on future generations.

After this comes the most famous passage of the whole book – the Shema – which every Jewish child still learns and in which the first commandment is expanded and anchored in everyday life.

> Hear, O Israel; The Lord our God, the Lord is one.
> Love the Lord your God with all your heart and
> with all your soul and with all your strength. These
> commandments that I give you today are to be
> upon your hearts. Impress them on your children.
> Talk about them when you sit at home and when
> you lie down and when you get up. Tie them as
> symbols on your hands and bind them on your
> foreheads. Write them on the frames of your
> houses and on your gates. [Deuteronomy 6:4-9]

For the Israelites then, as for orthodox Jews today, these instructions were part of the command and were to be taken literally. But I wonder if that was what Moses, or even God, really meant. Was it not that the word of the Lord was to be so much part of their lives that it was as if it was tied on their hands and painted on the gateposts? While today, most Christians would not apply this literally; we should be applying it creatively so that our homes and our lives are permeated by the presence of God and of his love for us and ours for him. The children should see from their surroundings that God is important to us. Returning to Deuteronomy;

> Take to heart all the words I have solemnly declared to you this day, so that you may command your children to obey carefully all the commands of this law. They are not just idle words for you – they are your life. [Deuteronomy 32: 46]

The commands God gives us are our life! They are *that* important. Because they are our life, they are life for our children too. They are more important than anything else we can put into their lives, because they are life bringing. We are careful to send the children to school, choosing the best we can for them. We take them to the dentist, get their injections done, teach them about road safety, and make sure they can swim. We teach them about the dangers of taking drugs, and what too much alcohol can do and we give them driving lessons. Then we say 'Oh, the Sunday school or youth group does a wonderful job – we can leave it to them,' or even worse, 'They can make their own minds up when they are old enough.'

We have to teach and show and demonstrate and indoctrinate and live the commands of God day by day for our children. God commands it – whatever society or modern political correctness says. Our obedience belongs to him. Indoctrination has become a dirty word – but doctrine is what we believe and obey and indoctrination is putting doctrine in. So yes, we should indoctrinate and be proud of it.

The passage in Deuteronomy goes on to say; 'when your son asks...tell him.' All the paintings, texts, Bibles, Christian books in the world will not be any more than wallpaper, unless their relevance and importance to our faith in God is explained. We call the Bible the Word of God. It is not – if by Bible we means the actual book, the paper and the printed words. It is only the word of God when he speaks it, into our lives and hearts. It becomes the Word of God when it speaks to us. God speaks to us and to our children through the ins and outs of daily life. We have to speak his words and his praise to our children. Psalm 78; 4 'We will tell the next generation the praiseworthy deeds of the Lord.'

God commands us to communicate with our children – and specifically to tell them about him – the eternal changeless truth about who he is, the exciting new ways he is dealing with us, our excitement at belonging to him and our love and dependence on him. If this life with God is not real or important to us, we will not be able to communicate it to the children. We cannot fool our children. If church on Sunday is all there is to our faith, there will be nothing to share. Only what is real and important to us is what the children absorb from us and this absorption comes more by shared life than by direct teaching. So my son absorbed a love of football from his dad, and played in school teams all through his childhood. Now, grown and married, he still plays football and enjoys going to a football match to watch the local team with his dad when he comes for a visit. Both my children love music, because they were surrounded with music before birth, and encouraged to make it for themselves from soon after. The reality – or not – of our life with God is what will impact – or not – our children. Somehow we have to learn how to communicate the reality of our God to our children. Faith is like measles – if they don't come into contact with it, they won't catch it. What we communicate is what they inherit.

So we need to reclaim our concept of being holy and set apart for God. There is a verse where God says 'I will not give my glory to another'. We cannot neglect him in our daily lives and expect him to bless us with faithful believing children.

But God also commands us to discipline our children. Commanded to discipline? Yes, but let's get clear on what discipline means. It's not simply punishment, though occasionally it might be. The word discipline has the same root as disciple. Discipline is 'making a disciple'. The dictionary definition is 'training that is expected to produce a particular character or pattern of behaviour, especially that which is expected to produce moral or mental improvement, a systematic method of obtaining such behaviour.' There is structure and purpose in discipline. The Bible tells us that it is the parents' job to discipline their children, to form them into disciples, to train them to be followers of Jesus. It is a command for parents. Discipline is a word that has various stages of meaning. We talk about the discipline of a certain course of study. We talk about discipline in the sense of physical training – a marathon runner will submit to the discipline of special diets and training schedules. The discipline in a school is what produces well-behaved, hardworking and polite students. Self-discipline is what makes a person choose to do one thing rather than another, for the sake of some future achievement. So my lack of self-discipline is what is hindering my learning of Croatian. The future achievement would be to be able to speak to my friends out there in their own language. Discipline is the only thing that will enable me to achieve that end. But then of course, when we refer to children we see discipline in negative terms. We have seen that it is necessary in our own lives – why then do we think that children can be raised – or even loved – without discipline? The Bible is quite clear that we – and our children need discipline.

> Discipline your son, for in that there is hope; do not be a willing party to his death. [Proverbs 19:18]

> Take to heart all the words … so that you may command your children to obey carefully. [Deuteronomy 32:46]

It may be hard work, it may cause struggles and battles within the family as the children try to take command, but that is no reason not to do what God tell us. The argument that children should be left alone to make up their own minds when they are older is contrary to Biblical parenting. We have a responsibility to our children to teach and train them in God's ways – just as he teaches and trains us. We have a responsibility to God, for he entrusted them to us to train for him. So we need to be accepting and obeying the discipline the Lord has taught us – we cannot discipline our children effectively unless we are self-disciplined.

Discipline, being dependent on relationship and communication, takes time. Discipline means knowing what is going on in the child's life so that he may be trained into goodness and protected from the bad. It is much easier to give in to whining and whingeing, to allow them to watch that x-rated video, or to stay out till midnight because 'everyone else will,' than to insist on obedience and alternatives. But discipline and love are the two sides of one coin. If we truly love our children, we will do our best to make them what they are capable of being. God sent Jesus to die for our sins, and his Spirit to conform us to his image; in the same way, we will have to sacrifice ourselves and serve our children, doing all we can to fashion them into his image through our representation to them of that image.

Interestingly, I could not find a verse in the Bible commanding us to love our children – not because we are not meant to, but because in the societies in which it was written, and surely in the mind of God, love for one's offspring is a given. He continues to love us even when we have refused to have anything to do with him. We are supposed, as Christians to love our children the same way. However as we see in our sad society today, this is not always the case. What passes for love may be no more than indulgence. Children who are constantly given in to, either emotionally or materially, are in fact love starved. Love is not easy; discipline is not negative. Discipline is part of love. Discipline is wanting the best for the child. Love is wanting the best for the child. Discipline is enabling the best to become possible.

So to sum up, a child's needs are for love, discipline and communication. All these can only be fed into the child's life through time. That is one reason God invented family; because family is the best way of giving these things to children. The church structure and leadership can also be part of the fulfilling of these needs and the more comfortable safe adults the child knows the more opportunity there is for these needs to be fully met. This is why open homes and community churches are so successful in keeping the teenagers – they know themselves loved and valued by many adults in such an environment. Children who are loved in this way, in a secure long-term environment, grow up confident and with a good sense of their own identity. Achieving this for our children takes time. It takes faithfulness. It means sacrifice. But as they grow they also need a vision. Our God has the biggest vision the world has – world dominion! Let's get them hitched in to that!

The problem with this, in our busy fragmented modern lifestyle, is that communication takes time. If we have children we have to make time to share the important things with them, and take time to enjoy the trivial fun times together. Do you remember the story Jesus told about the man who wanted to borrow a loaf of bread from his neighbour? What was the neighbour's response? 'Don't bother me. The door is already locked and my children are already in bed with me. I can't get up and give you anything.' [Luke 11:7]. It was family time – Dad, Mum and the kids, all together, talking through the day, thanking God for the good things and asking his blessing for the night. This is the way it was in first century Israel; small houses inevitably brought closeness and communication. It is not necessarily so today. With one or both parents working, and separate rooms for sleeping, and television and computers to provide an alternative focus, there is less time for togetherness. But we can't communicate God to our children if we are not there, or if they are not there, or if the television always is! If you are too busy for time with your children then you are too busy! As Christians we are the children of a God of relationship. People are always more important than things. This is not a plea to return to the 'traditional mum at home with the kids and dad out at work earning the money' kind of family – which is in fact far from traditional and has hardly ever existed throughout history. The Bible is remarkably silent about the roles of husband and wife. It does not say whether being a working mother is a valid role for Christians today. Or to be a 'househusband'! Which implies very strongly that this is not the issue. What it does tell us is that man and wife together are the normal basis for family, and both have a role in bringing up the children. The father's role Biblically is much greater than we today tend to allow – his is the primary role for teaching about God.

Throughout history the most common family work pattern has been for all the family members, as they are able, to contribute to the family business. Father leaving home for the major part of every day to work at something unknown and alien to his family is historically a fairly recent phenomenon. So we might just as well say that all Christians fathers must become self-employed and work at home, as that all Christian mothers must work at it full time! The simple fact is that each 21st century Christian family must work out from many options what works for them and what proportion of time should be spent at home and what at work, for each adult member. The children's needs for time and care must always be uppermost in the planning but no one has the right to dictate to anyone else. But please, if you are very busy, and most of us are these days, check from time to time to make sure your priorities are still right.

Are you still able to give enough time to your children? If we are putting all our energies into work or church, what are we communicating to our children? That they come very low on our agenda? That their spiritual needs are less important than those of adults? That God doesn't really care about them as much as he does about the grownups? Children know when they are second best. They know if Dad really loves them or if he's really too busy being important at church. 'Children's questions must be taken seriously at the age of two and three or they won't be continuing to ask you at twelve or twenty-three.' [*What is a family?* Edith Schaeffer. Hodder 1975] If we push them away when they are little, they will learn that we are not really interested; then when they are making life changing decisions in their teens, it will be their friends they consult, not us. The most important task Christian parents have is bringing their children up to be strongly committed Christian teenagers and young people. Both parents if both are available. And as many other interested adults of all ages as can be persuaded to be involved. We need to make time to get to know our children, to be part of their lives, and to teach them the wonderful things about God that we want them to know.

Chapter Ten

What the Teenagers Need

'I just want to be treated like an adult.'

'I'm not a child any more.'

'You never listen.'

'You don't understand.'

'Don't treat me like a child.'

If you are a parent of teenage children, you have probably had at least one of these retorts thrown at you in the course of a conversation. Teenagers want to be treated as adults. We look at them and see children. This differing viewpoint is an argument waiting to happen. How do we avoid this? We need perhaps to remember that today in the West, 'childhood' lasts longer than it has at any other time in history. Jesus was considered an adult member of society, like every Jewish boy at that time, at twelve when he had his Bar Mitzvah. Children of twelve and thirteen used to be considered old enough to marry. Yet these days, eighteen is becoming more and more the normal age for leaving school, and even them increasing numbers of young people are continuing into further full time education, thereby delaying their entry into the adult world of work by another three or four years. No wonder they sometimes get frustrated. Yet at other times, it seems that they want to be children again. A friend of mine, both of whose sons, now in their twenties are strong Christians, had these wise words to say,

> Children are the same as adults. Only difference is that they are smaller and lack training and experience. So far as possible offer them the benefit of your experience but don't force it on them. You won't always be around so they need training in making up their own minds. Start early. Rule 1. The child is not there for your benefit, you are there for his.

What the teenagers need is to be treated in a way that respects them as a person, while still continuing the training and modelling that began in early childhood. Communication remains vital but so does love. Discipline should be moving from adult imposed to self imposed but the way and speed this happens will obviously vary from family to family and even child to child. Mutual respect and understanding should be growing as the child progresses through the teenage years.

But I think the most important thing we can do for our teenagers is to realise how important it is that our faith is lived out at home. If we are consistently Christian at home with them, and seeing them as part of the covenant people, many of the difficulties we see today will disappear.

Christianity is a lifestyle. Jesus said, ' I am the Way,' and his followers took up this word as a description of themselves. Long before they were 'Christians' they were 'followers of the Way' [Acts

9:2, 24:14] God has always been concerned about how his people behave! In Exodus he moves from demanding their undivided allegiance [Exodus 20:3] to commanding them to control their desires for what their neighbours owned. [20:17] 'Worship me and don't even think about fancying your neighbour's wife.' When we take our faith out of day-to-day life, we kill our faith. It is only as we live that we prove who – or what – we worship. If you really want to know what is important in your life, work out what you spend most time at – either thinking about or doing.

Jesus spent hours teaching his disciples how to get on with each other. Do you think James and John, the 'sons of thunder', may still have been in their teens? It might explain the nickname. Paul wrote letter after letter doing the same thing! James' letter, where we read, 'Faith by itself, if it not accompanied by action, is dead' [James 2: 17], is proof that the early Christians, even Jesus' own brother, saw the need for behaviour to reflect profession. New Testament teaching is about how to live in relationship. It is about living out our faith in community, worshipping God in daily life. It is about balancing grace and obedience so that we offer unconditional love while demanding our 'utmost for his highest'. Do we, when we read what I call the lifestyle parts of the epistles, do we consciously apply them to our life within the four walls of our home? 'You, my brothers, were called to be free. But do not use your freedom to indulge the sinful nature, rather, serve one another in love.'[Galatians 5:13]. This comes after a discussion about what freedom in Christ really consists of. Suddenly we are in the realm of daily life. Spiritual freedom is demonstrated in physical life. But do we apply this to our relationships with our teenagers?

If we have taken seriously the fact that God is committed to us as a family, not just as individuals, if his covenant is with the whole community, then these awkward teenagers are part of that and we need to treat them as if they are. If God's claim is on the whole of our lives and if our children's salvation to some extent is influenced by our obedience surely it is partly because the way we treat them either pulls them towards God or pushes them further away from him. If we are living out the commands of the Bible, we must be doing so at home with regard to our teenagers. Just as charity begins at home, so must holiness.

It is time for radical discipleship, not just more of the same way of life with a veneer of Christianity tacked on. We have compromised too long with the world's way of doing things and as a result are powerless to make changes in the world or even in our families. The early Christians on the other hand, did not even need to specify what 'Way' they were following; everyone could see that for them there only was one way – the Way of Christ.

When we read the epistles we see that the majority of the practical teaching in the Bible is to do with relationship. Our spiritual life can only be worked out in our physical life. There is no alternative. We don't know if we are gentle, faithful, kind, or self-controlled until life rubs up against us. It is how we react when the toddler spills his milk on the carpet for the fifth time in a week, or the teenager hasn't said anything to us except an untranslatable mumble for a month, that demonstrates how much the love of God is in us. It's easy to smile and be gentle and kind on Sunday morning for an hour in church, but what about Monday morning, when it's raining and the dog's been sick and the toast is burnt and the car won't start? Too often our lives do not match up to our profession, and that's why our children don't want to know. This seems to be worst for the children of Christian workers – 'Dad's always got time for others, but never for me' or they feel the pressure to match up to the church's expectations of 'the vicar's children'. But if the vicar explodes at them, or neglects them, he is living a lie and storing up pain for himself and his children. Our words and our lives must match up, and we can see that our faith should have a visible effect on the relationships we have within our own families, within the church community and towards the larger community in which we live.

God is calling us to look at our lifestyle at home and how this impacts on the next generation, as well as on our neighbours. We have seen how he claims those he covenants with as his own, and demands obedience as our part of that covenant. He lays claim to all of our lives. We dare not be one thing at home and another outside. For the sake of our children we need to teach but we also need to model. The children know God is loving, just, patient, fun to be with, full of good things, because their parents are. They know their heavenly Father loves them and has time for them because their earthly father does. They understand how forgiveness works because they both receive and give forgiveness in a family setting. They see something of God's holiness reflected in the way their parents live. They see God's welcoming inclusiveness when singles, strangers, wounded ones are invited into their homes. Whether we like it or not they will weigh up what we say we believe and if our actions at home with them deny it, they will reject it. If you are not Christian at home in your dealings with your family members then you are not Christian.

The distinctiveness of the church only comes when we live a kingdom lifestyle, not when we tell them what we believe is true, whether 'them' is our own teenagers or people who live around us. There are many voices, all claiming to have the truth for now. Most people are not interested in absolute truth, what they want is a truth to live by, now, at this moment, in this crisis. They don't want us to tell them the truth, they want reality. Reality is truth with flesh on. They don't need teaching what church is; they need showing. They have looked at church and seen hypocrisy; we have got to learn to model authenticity. Belief in Jesus must not ever, be just an intellectual assent to a set of truths; we all say it, but for many of us that is exactly what our faith is. It's reduced to a set of facts that we believe, and has no effect at all on our lifestyle or character. What church needs is a lifestyle change. What our teenagers need from us is a lifestyle that reflects faithfully the things we say and preach on Sundays. They need to see that our lives and our beliefs are consistent, and that they are effective.

Jesus told us to love one another. Love, the way he meant it, is commitment, sharing, laughing, eating, crying, suffering together. It's putting up with foibles, giving up our own preferences, tolerating difference and encouraging potential. It's interfamily, intergenerational. It's old people and children, babies and teenagers. It's finding unity in diversity. It's breaking down all the barriers, especially the generational one. It's realising we all need each other, and can learn and worship *together*. It's time consuming. It's hard work. It's costly. It's painful. But it's necessary. It is also fun and excitement and creativity. It's about sharing lives. We need to share our lives with other Christians because it is only in fellowship that our Christian faith can be worked out. We cannot do any of this is we continue to live with our front doors firmly closed and our homes only allowing in the members of the nuclear family living there. Openness is important, for the world's sake, but also for our children's sake. But the most important person we must let into our homes is of course Jesus himself. We need him living in us and in our homes before we can share him with others.

'Can I ask you something?' Martin came hesitantly into the lounge where I was sitting reading.

'Of course.'

'Well, how is it you are all so nice to each other? I thought you were putting it on because I was staying, but no one could keep it up for this long.'

Martin, age twenty, had been staying with us for a month. He was Swiss and had driven us nearly mad with his constant comparison of all things English with all things Swiss, to the vast disparagement of the former. Many a night we had escaped into our bedroom, exploded to each other and prayed for patience – specifically not to explode at him! What lay behind his question was that fact that his own, Christian, father treated him in a domineering manner, expecting instant obedience and subservience. Martin, it turned out, was never allowed to have an opinion of his own. He was amazed at the open friendliness there was in our family and his rather objectionable behaviour had been designed to test its strength and validity.

The ensuing conversation went along the lines of yes, we could be that nice to each other, because Jesus was the one we all obeyed and loved. He asked what would happen if the children disagreed with us about anything, and seemed amazed when I said I'd be quite happy for them to support a different political party, for example. He then wanted to know if there were things the children couldn't talk to us, their parents, about. I said I didn't think so, but he'd have to ask them. He did, and bless them, they said they could talk to us about anything! At the time my children were 14 and 16 – difficult ages. We were not, and still are not, a perfect family; but we are a family where grace and love operate, thanks only to the Lord. Martin had seen a Christian family who were trying to put the teaching in the epistles into practice, and who were relying on grace, mercy and forgiveness, from God originally but also extended to each other. What he saw attracted him to want it for himself. Notice how he tested it first. He had been short-changed in his own concept of what Christianity is and how it works and he wasn't going to be taken in by anything that wasn't real. The experience was also encouraging to my own children's faith, as they saw the reality of what they believed used to help someone else.

That incident was a picture of church at work – people coming face to face with the reality of Jesus in day-to-day life, and the glory going to him. Martin went home to Switzerland, leaving us at the airport with a tear jerking last comment – 'I know now what I want when I get married.' A few months later we received a card with the verse written, 'In the last days, God says, I will pour out my Spirit on all people. Your sons and your daughters will prophecy, your young men will see visions.' Martin had added simply, 'I know this is true, I've seen it'.

The media tell us that parents have no influence on their children. They claim that children are more influenced by peer pressure, and the media. Well, they would say that, wouldn't they? But if you ask young people in church what the greatest influence in their own coming to faith is, they will more often than not say that it was their parents, or their home life. (Interestingly, not their church or their youth leader, though these are acknowledged to have played a significant part). In 'The Gospel According to Generation X' a survey of American young people, it is stated, 'Over three quarters of our kids say that their parents are the most important spiritual influence in their lives.' David Gelman, quoted in the same book says, 'Sociologists have begun to realize in fact that teens are shaped more by their parents than by their peers, that they adopt their parents' values and opinions to a greater degree than realized.' They are only realizing what the Bible already told us; 'Train a child in the way he should go, and when he is old he will not turn from it.' [Proverbs 22: 6].

What a tragedy then, that so many Christian parents leave the spiritual training to church or worse, leave the children with no training until they are 'old enough to decide for themselves'. Do you really want to leave the most important training to other people, or to chance? Isn't worshipping Jesus the most important thing in your life? And if it is, doesn't it affect the way you do *everything*? Christian parent, if it isn't and if it doesn't, are you surprised your children turn their backs on it?

Why did our family have such an effect on Martin? Not because we were perfect, but because the life of Jesus was worked out in our home. Our faith was not just a Sunday faith, put on with the smart church clothes and Sunday roast, and then left while we got on with the day-to-day affairs of life. It was a faith interwoven with everything we did. But he only saw it because we opened our home to him.

The church building is where God's people come together to meet God. They meet for united worship, teaching, friendship and support. The writer to Hebrews stresses the importance of regular, habitual meeting – 'Let us not give up meeting together, as some are in the habit of doing, but let us encourage each other – and all the more as you see the Day approaching.' [Hebrews 10:2]). In an increasingly centralized and impersonal society, we need the sense of being part of a worshipping community. Our children need that too – they need a good group of peers who are growing up the same way they are and finding out about Jesus together. Worship is important for those already in, but the disaffected ones and their friends and our neighbours are not actually rushing into church buildings to be inspired and challenged by our vibrant heartfelt worship. They will, however, come into our homes, particularly if there is food on offer!

It is in our homes that they can see the outworking of our worship because it is in the home that worship is expressed as practical day-to-day living. No home is perfect, but home should be the place where we live our faith and model Jesus. Home, not church, is the primary place where Christian values are caught and taught. It is in daily life that sacrificial, unconditional and inclusive love is shown. It is in relationship with others that the life of Jesus is expressed. Faith is worked out in business and family life.

When the apostles were writing their letters to the early church they were writing to people who, often, only met in homes. They were writing into the daily life of the followers of Jesus. Their instructions were for daily life, in the marketplace, the fields and the home. Their messages for us should also be applied in this way. We need to see that commands such as 'do everything without complaining or arguing' [Philippians 2:14] or 'as God's chosen people, holy and dearly loved, clothe yourselves with compassion, humility, gentleness and patience' [Colossians 3:12] are to be worked out at home in our most basic relationships, not just among our friends at church.

The epistles were written in a society where community was very important. The distinguishing mark of the early Christians was that they loved each other. This love also cut across the traditional societal barriers. Thus we get the letter of Paul to Philemon, asking him to love his slave as a brother because he is now part of the family of Christ. I don't think we are expected to think that Onesimus became any less Philemon's slave, but that a mutual respect and love occurred where before, reading between the lines, there was laziness and resentment. Go through the epistles and see how much of the teaching there is about relationship – getting on with each other, coping with differences, showing love and concern, being self-controlled. Imagine the difference it would make if the whole church took this on board and begin to live in it their families.

Now imagine the whole church opening their homes to the solitary, the weak and the lonely and the hurt. Church in community – day to day the life of the Kingdom flowing in and out of our homes. Wouldn't it be wonderful? When faith is tied up intricately with daily life the children will find it much harder to leave behind in their childhood.

Chapter Eleven

Aspects of Life with God

The central theme of this book is that God is committed to us, his people, not just, or even principally as individuals but also as a covenant community within which his kingdom life and values can be demonstrated, and that this covenant involves both width and depth. This covenant life is expressed both in our corporate worship at church and in our life at home, and finds its full expression when the two are complementary and in harmony. God promises that his love will continue down the generations if we obey him and thus his covenant now includes our children and their children. If he is committed to us like that, we should live in the light of that commitment and our lifestyle should reflect back our commitment to him. We have briefly discussed the need for radical commitment and the needs of children and teenagers with regard to this commitment. Now we are going to look at some specific issues that are raised by the culture we live in. We live in a culture which is primarily recognisable by its twin values of consumerism and individualism. The church and its families need to model a different way, a community way. This chapter will look at a few of the issues that radical Christian living will involve us making decisions on. These are not the only issues but are representative and are ones that most families have to make decisions about at some time. How we think about these things, as everything else, can have a great effect on whether or not our children follow us into faith.

Open homes

I was chatting to my grown-up daughter the other day. She has been away from home now for two years and is newly returned. On Saturday she said to me, 'Who's coming to lunch tomorrow?' Then she went on to say that one of her best memories from childhood, and something she wants to copy when she has her own home, is the habit of having people round for Sunday lunch, or visiting them. She said she couldn't really remember Sundays when we didn't have a shared meal with another family or families. Sharing meals, on Sunday lunchtime, or at any other time, is a good way of sharing lives. Families learn that other people do things differently, eat different food, and have different opinions. Children learn to relate to other people of all ages.

This sharing of meals is not the only way to have an open home. In the church my children grew up in, many families had extra people living with them for long or short periods. We have had, during the children's growing years, foreign visitors over here to learn English before going on the mission field, ex drug addicts, young singles, and extra children. I know it added a vital extra dimension to my own children's life but I hadn't seen this a generally significant factor until I spoke to other Christian families from many different situations where the children had grown into faith. Many parents said that they thought the extra people they had staying either long or short term were important to their children's development. Many young people said how they had gained from having other people in their homes. A surprisingly large proportion of the families I have talked to whose children grew up into faith, could look back to at least part of the children's childhood when the family included extra, unrelated members. Is it that more grace, more unconditional love is needed when the family includes 'strangers' and this cannot work without the Spirit's enabling? Or is it that seeing other adults believing the same faith strengthens and supports growing faith? But also at a purely social level learning to adjust to other people, to tolerate their different way of doing things is valuable at any age, but particularly when young.

Friendships

We invite our adult friends in for meals; do we welcome our children's friends in the same way? It is difficult when standards are different and we maybe don't even like the child very much, but persevering will have one of two results. Either the visiting child will over time adapt its behaviour to something which is acceptable, or you child will gradually see that this particular friend is not one that 'fits'. Either way, our job as representatives of Christ is to show welcoming and affirming love. You do not know if you are the only person who ever speaks to that child without using swear words! As the children grow up, I believe it is even more important for their friends to visit and to feel welcome. When they enter their teenage years we have much less influence over who their friends are, and if we don't know them, we cannot influence either them or our own child. There are many teenagers today, who if they do not have access into a Christian home, will never have the experience of seeing a full two parent family working and living together happily and successfully. This model may be just what they need to enable them to make strong lasting relationships when they grow up. 84% of generation Xers, according to Christian Research, believe marriage should be for life, despite the fact that a lot of them come from broken or dysfunctional homes.

Do not underestimate the power of a house where Jesus lives. For too long we have assumed that our children are inevitably going to be adversely influenced if they make 'unsuitable' friends. Let us begin to believe that they, being infilled by the Spirit of God, dedicated to him, and protected by his covenant, could be the ones doing the influencing. Love is attractive; the power of God to change lives is impressive, and our children can be used to extend the kingdom. Our children do have the ability to be influences for good. But we need to know what is going on – their friendships do need to be both monitored and open. Praying with and for them about their friends shows that we consider this part of their lives important. Hannah, age 16, is going to New Zealand on a millennium trip. As far as she knows she is the only Christian going. So she and her parents and the church are praying that she will be strengthened and that she will be an influence for good and for God among those young people, that her faith will grow as a result of this experience. (She's back, and it did!)

As adults who are part of a church community, we need also to look at our own friendships. We need other Christians with whom we share our lives, but we also need to be friends with those as yet outside. There is also an opportunity to say something about 'singles'. The church should be a place where 'the singles are set in families', not just by the families inviting the single, but also the other way round. An unmarried adult can add an extra dimension to a teenager's life, but young people can also be a breath of fresh air to the single adult, not least because they are not yet tied into the couple mentality.

Independence

This discussion of friendship leads us onto a consideration of independence. We hear a lot about the need to let young people be independent, but what does that mean in our situation? As the people of God we are not meant to be independent but dependent on him. Between complete independence and dependence on God there is all the difference in the world.

Why do our young people need independence and what do they need it from and for? Our children are in our care and as such they do need to be protected from real danger, while being given the skills and self-confidence to go out into the world and be safe. We do, while they are living in our house, need to know who they are with and where they are. Though even here, my friend with the two sons mentioned earlier, had this to say, 'Don't be overprotective. I see little value in a parent insisting on knowing where the child is all the time: it's more sensible to make sure that the child knows where you are so that he can call for help if needed.' We need to know who the children's friends are and whether we approve. If we don't and the children are in their teenage years prayer is both more practical and less confrontational than a veto. This of course, is where an open home, and the habit of encouraging children to bring their friends home, pays dividends.

But we do not, as suggested was the case in a television programme the other week, all need to read our children's correspondence and diaries. They need growing privacy as they grow up. They also need grow up into self-reliance rather than reliance on their parents. Confidence in our own ability to survive within our world is important. To borrow a phrase that I first read as the title of Elizabeth Gibson's book about her own family life, we need to give our teenagers both roots and wings. Roots, to know who they are and where they have come from, and to know that whatever happens they will still have a place in our love to return to. Wings, to fly wide and safely into their future. But it is possible to give them too much independence too soon. There was a story in the paper about a brother and sister of ten and twelve both of whom were sexually active, and whose mother said it was normal and to be expected. Too much freedom too soon. Thirteen-year-old children whose parents don't know where they are and who steal cars and get into drugs. Too much freedom, too soon.

Sixteen year olds who go to Africa for a month to build a house for a mission compound. The right kind of independence.

One of the things we need to consider is this issue of control versus independence, not only for the children or the young people but also for the adults. We are hearing, at least in my church, more of the concept of accountability within the wider church context. As God's people, we are in relationship with each other and have to work out the relative values of independence and mutual dependence within our desire to love and model Jesus' way of living.

Attitude to wealth

In the West Christians seem to be confused about money and wealth. The prosperity gospel tells us that God wants us all rich, while other people seem to believe that Christians shouldn't enjoy material prosperity. But our ability to create wealth is God given and some Christians should be at the top of their professions – because as Christians we should work better, more efficiently, more honestly and more creatively. Nowhere does the Bible say that money is evil; the often misquoted verse in Timothy actually says:

> The love of money is a root of all kinds of evil.
> Some people, eager for money, have wandered
> from the faith and pierced themselves with many
> griefs. [1 Timothy 6:10]

Clearly if money is our goal it's an idol. This is a danger to which we in the affluent West are prone. How do we know that we are not idolizing our money? The young people often throw this criticism at the church, that we say we trust in God but actually trust in our own ability to make and save money. As society strives for more and better everything, maybe it's time for us to become much more vocal in enjoying what we've got, and giving God the glory for it. When the Israelites were about to enter the Promised Land, Moses said this to them:

> When you have eaten and are satisfied, praise the Lord your God for the good land he has given you. Be careful that you do not forget the Lord your God … Otherwise when you eat and are satisfied, when you build fine houses and settle down, and when your flocks and herds grow large, and your silver and gold increase, and all you have is multiplied, then your heart will become proud and you will forget the Lord your God.
> [Deuteronomy 8:10, 12-14]

For us enjoying has to mean sharing, giving away. Jesus moved easily from a homeless wandering existence where they had not even the money needed to pay tax without taking it from the mouth of a fish, to feasting with the rich tax collector and entertaining influential Pharisees. The Bible tells us that all of this world's goodness is given from God and as such we are not meant to be ungrateful, nor are we meant to grasp and cling to it. But we live in a society that sees security in financial terms and it is therefore very difficult to go counter to this. But as Christians surely we should use material gifts to give pleasure to others and to reflect the way God showers good things on us. It is not good for children to have everything they want – just as it is not good for us. It is not good for us or them to see what we have as our right or our possession.

There was a small girl in our church. She was told of another little girl whose house had caught fire and been completely destroyed with all its contents, She was asked if she had any toys to give to the child who had lost everything. She immediately ran to her room and brought out her favourite doll with all its clothes. When asked why she had brought her favourite doll she replied, ' I've got lots of others, but this is the only one she'll have so I want it to be the best.' That child had learnt to hold her possessions lightly – and she wasn't immediately bought a new doll to replace the one she had given away!

Faith and risk taking

What do the children see in their parents? A boring middle-aged (old?) couple who never do anything exciting? Or people actively working with God on new and strange adventures? Our children grew up involved with a drug rehabilitation centre – and among other things, learnt to eat cabbage and liver (both of which they hated) because that's what there was for supper there. Whatever you think of Jesus' lifestyle it wasn't either boring or conventional. How much his mother must have wished that he would stay at home and carry on the carpenter's business! But Jesus walked into dangerous situations, and out the other side, having transformed them. We should do the same. An active, missionary faith will inspire the same in our children. Where do the children see our security lying? If it is in money, pension plans, promotion at work, they will probably reject our claims that we rely on God for security. If our financial security and our spiritual security reside in two different places, we have missed the point of what Jesus came to do. Taking risks for God with our money or our time or our future demonstrates that we have faith in the God we follow.

Freedom versus rules

A wise Christian once said, 'Love God and do what you like'. Wouldn't it be nice if we all loved God so much that the right thing was always what we wanted to do? David, the psalmist expressed in slightly differently ' Delight yourself in the Lord and he will give you the desires of your heart.' But we are not yet perfect, though holy in his sight, and so we need rules. But these need to be as few and as clearly expressed as possible. Then they need to be insisted on. No matter how many tantrums, arguments or tears are produced. The reason for rules is discipline. The aim of discipline is self-discipline. The purpose of any kind of discipline is order and growth. Behaviour can be legislated for, thought can't; we can tell our children how to behave, we cannot tell them how to think. Rules bring the need for sanctions – to slap or not to slap, and if not to slap, how to punish. This is another area where we may find that modern political correctness and what the Bible says seem to be at odds, and we each need to work out our own way of living with that tension. But children are supposed to obey their parents and parents are not supposed to exasperate their children. [See Ephesians 6:1-4]

Balance of love and discipline

This is an area we have already looked at in some depth, so we here need do no more than recap briefly. Love and discipline are the two sides of one coin. It seems more loving to let a child do what he wants, but it isn't. Discipline is not abuse or only punishment. Discipline is training. Love must be part of discipline as discipline must be part of love. Love must also be shown – said and demonstrated. Love is made concrete in time shared; the most important thing you can give your children as they grow through their teenage years is time. The few minutes before bed are a wonderful time for sharing and praying together. In the car is another good place. But make sure the channels of communication are kept open; once they close, even for a few months, it is difficult to force them open again.

Family loyalty and commitment

There are very few things that God says he hates in the Bible. Divorce is one of them. Why? Because one of God's characteristics is faithfulness. He is committed to us forever. We are supposed to reflect that characteristic. So divorce really is not an option – it's not even in the picture – when two people are truly committed to God and determined to live his way. So family loyalty starts with the parents. No marriage is perfect. No marriage is flawless. There are times in every relationship when it seems easier to give up and walk away. But working through difficulties brings greater strength and maturity. It also protects the children from the insecurity and crises of identity that children of divorce inevitably have to cope with.

Family loyalty also means that just as the parents are committed to each other forever, they are committed to the children no matter what. We have to have the same unconditional love for our children that God has for us. No sin is too great for his forgiveness and equally there can be nothing that our children will do that can stop us loving and forgiving them. This does not mean we condone any kind of behaviour. If we want our children to be the best they can for God we have to insist on their best for us. But we forgive when they fail to live up to it.

Every child grows up with the feeling that they way their family does things is the right way. It is not till they have visited friends and talked to schoolmates that they realize that it is possible to do things differently and still be a loving family. This is one reason why open homes are so important. Not only do our children see other models of living, both actively Christian and not, but also children from nonchristian homes see real Christianity for themselves. So, for example, grace before meals is an important declaration of whose we are. But it is also children of broken or dysfunctional homes who can see and be drawn to something of the love of God for themselves – they would be very unlikely to be drawn to a church without the intermediary knowledge and love of a Christian family. This is a role which must become more and more important as society fragments increasingly.

Church loyalty
Church should never be the most important thing in a family's life – God should. Church must be a

place where children as well as adults feel they belong, and are valued and loved. The security of growing up into adulthood within one church community can be tremendous. When a child who has been through the crèche and the Sunday school and the youth group leaves for university, he knows all those who have been involved throughout his childhood will be praying for him. When he comes home there will be people who welcome him back and want to know how he got on. However for many teenagers growing up involves choosing to worship at a different church on in a different style from their parents and the church they grew up in. It is easy to see this as a kind of betrayal whereas in fact it is no more than an expression of personal preference and independence. I would far rather my children went to a youth church than a nightclub! Even if both are equally noisy.

Commitment to outreach

God is committed to mission. As his people we should be too. A family is not meant to be a closed unit either. People who come into the family for a while as non-believers can go out again as part of the family of faith. Once again open homes provide both the setting and the opportunity for mission, but children can also be encouraged to support missionaries overseas with letters and emails and prayer. They can also be involved in their own mission activities. There was a group of children ranging from twelve to six years who, over a period of three years collected well over three hundred pounds for children's missions by making and selling craft items and putting on concerts. They were encouraged by their parents but the motivation and ideas all came from the children themselves. Incidentally they learnt about cash flow and book keeping! Mission can be both entertaining and educational.

Technology

We live in a world where technology is literally everywhere. We claim not to be dependent on it, but we only have to experience a power cut, and we realize that we are not as independent as we think! Ours is an electronic age; our children use computers almost as soon as they are born. Christians must be able to use and develop these technologies. Television, computers and other technological wonders are morally neutral. They can bring good things into our lives or they can be a channel of unbelievable evil. While our children are small we need to protect from the evil and as they grow teach them to be wise and discerning. If we, as committed Christian parents, with a God given authority over our children, allow things to happen or appear which dishonour God or glorify the opposition, we are at fault – it is our sin. We have lost our zeal for God's honour. The children will reap the harvest of our sin.

It is wise to be aware that all this technology uses up time and prevents socializing. Each family needs to work out its own rules and strategies towards the use of personal computers, televisions and phones. But we also need to thank God for them; we can keep in touch so much more easily and learn things so much more conveniently as a result of discovery of the microchip. As Christians the one thing we should not do is have a reactionary fear of new technology because it too is a part of God's creation and we should be using it for his glory. Our problem, as with so many things, is to work out a balance that glorifies God and works towards a healthy harmonious and committed lifestyle for our family.

Celebration

The children of Israel knew how to party! Among other things they celebrated Passover, Pentecost, New year, Tabernacles; all according to God's instructions.

> Celebrate the Feast of Tabernacles for seven days after you have gathered the produce of your threshing floor and your winepress. Be joyful at your feast – you, your sons and daughters ...[Deuteronomy 16:17]

They also kept the Sabbath. Many of the families I asked about what they put down the success of their children coming to faith mentioned among other things that Sunday was a special or different day. Many also said the insistence on attendance at church was also a significant factor. This goes against the received wisdom that expecting children to attend church pushes them away. (I think we have to assume however that these families had found a church community where their children were accepted and had friends of their own.) But keeping one day special, as a 'God, family and friends day' seems to be a major factor for many young people in growing up into faith. Celebration of the good things of life is also something that the church community can and should model.

One family in our church held a firework party last November. They invited the families in their street. Many people commented on how nice it was to have all the ages enjoying the evening together – teenagers, small children, parents and grandparents. This is something that seems to happen less and less frequently as each group has its own way of enjoying itself. But the generations can have fun together, and Christian families are the ones who are ideally placed to show them how to do this. Relationship is built through such activities both within and without the family. Bonfire night and Halloween are times when Christian families can demonstrate that we know how to enjoy ourselves and have fun, all together, and in the case of the latter, offer something considerably more wholesome than what the children would find elsewhere. But our celebrations should not be nothing more than thinly disguised excuses for evangelism – genuine and sincere enjoyment of God's gifts and the people who are sharing them with us has a value and attraction of its own which is more compelling and less cringe making for us and our teenagers!

From these few discussions we can see that living out our commitment to our covenant giving God, and applying the teaching in the New Testament on relationships has to affect every aspect of our life. Every family, every household has to make its own decisions but it is important that they are founded on a desire to live a life in line with God's will. If our lives are committed to God, fulfilled, exciting, challenging and demanding then I think, rather than continuing to lose our teenagers from the church, we will be seeing others, and their parents flooding in to become part of this loving dynamic community.

Part four

Healthy circulation restored?

Proving the generation gap is not a
black hole!

Chapter Twelve

Church in Community

'I don't want to go to church – it's boring.' I wonder how many times words like these have been said in houses throughout England. Your teenagers may say it out loud, but how often has this thought been in your mind as well as you climb into the car on Sunday morning. For all of us, church can seem a million miles away from the problems and decisions of day-to-day life. For the teenagers it can often seem not only miles away but also centuries away. We have looked at ways of living our faith in a generational covenant keeping God out in our daily life, but how does church attendance relate? If church is boring and remote what can we do about it? How do we make it relevant and compelling for them? Are there some churches that have got it right? Is there one kind of church that has the answer to keeping its teenagers? Does a single denomination have the solution?

The good news is that according to the Christian Research Organisation's finding it doesn't really seem to matter whether your church is Baptist, Anglican or Catholic. The bad news is that each denomination seems to fail as much as the next. But scattered through the different styles and names of churches there are examples of churches where faith is transmitted successfully down through the generations. It is not denomination but life that matters. Our teenagers are growing up not just in families but also in churches – and the kind of church they are in has a very definite effect on their continuing or not in faith through into adulthood. So the topic of keeping the children as they grow up is not just relevant to parents but also to church leaders. In any church the children's work is vital – without it the church dies. Equally, church attendance is a vital part in the children's growth into adult faith. Unfortunately it can often be a huge stumbling block instead. But this does not have to be the case.

Imagine a new housing estate with 1000 houses on the edge of a large town. Scattered among the families in those houses are a few Christians, who Sunday by Sunday get in their cars and drive to churches all over the town. Gradually they get to know each other and start a children's work. A Bible club after school in three houses on the estate involves the younger children, then a coffee morning for mums and preschool children is added. This grows to monthly Sunday services in the local school, then weekly, and a church is born. A church that intended always to be a community church serving and loving the people living in the area. We had no full time workers, the church was owned by everyone who was part of it, and when the time came for a building, in the centre of the estate, it was literally built by the men of the church, and some who weren't at the start but belonged, and believed, by the end of the building process. It was prayed into being and kept safe by the consistent prayer of a group of older people living in their own homes and in the sheltered housing on the estate. The older children joined in and helped and the younger ones did their bit by bringing a picnic lunch along for the workers, and staying to share it. While the men were building the church the women were building family – the older people from the sheltered housing were included, visited, loved, taken shopping, used as babysitters, and generally provided another layer of adult attention for a whole generation of children. Working mums knew that their children would go home from school to a house where other children were; where homework, television, afterschool activities, drinks and tea would happen just as if they were in their own homes. Meanwhile their contribution to the world of work was valued, prayed for and they were able to continue knowing their children were not being neglected. Children knew they were welcome in any of ten or so houses, for meals, sleepovers, chats, Bible clubs, music groups.

Clothes were recycled to such an extent that we could have put Mothercare out of business; my daughter's clothes, handed down to her from an older friend, then went through at least three younger children before finally giving up, and a favourite topic of conversation on Sundays before the service started was, 'Who's was this *first*?' Lest you think this was all too idyllic, it wasn't just nice cosy middle class church – we had spiky haired petrol sniffers coming to the youth group (on condition they hadn't been sniffing when they arrived on the door step). There were many housing association houses on the estate and we often had children watching the services in the church from vantage points high in the trees around the edge of the site, before deciding to hang around by the doorway, and eventually after many weeks make their way just through the door to the bench at the back. There were many old and lonely people living in the sheltered housing who found a new family and a reason to live again in the children of the church who regularly visited and also invited them to activities at their schools and clubs. The homes were not just open to other members of the church either, one family regularly hosted foreign students learning English before going onto the mission field, another fostered children, a third gave respite care for a Downs syndrome child, yet another welcomed an elderly lady into their home to live. The teenagers had their youth group in a family home, and as they arrived on Bible study nights, enjoyed the bedtime ritual of the toddlers – who thought everyone there needed a goodnight kiss! The toddlers parents enjoyed the luxury of twenty ready made and willing baby sitters whom the children already knew, and who later, on babysitting nights taught the little ones to play marbles and draw in perspective.

There were single-parent families whose children learnt it was fun to play rounders with everyone, other people's dads included, and who found a male role model lacking in their own homes. In those same rounders games and picnics the young men learnt to relate easily to small children too. Living on a modern housing estate with walkways and car free areas, meant that the children had more freedom than many, and were always in and out of each other's houses. Most of the church business went on in homes too, from home groups to youth groups, from Bible clubs to services. All this meant that church – and God – could not be divorced from daily life – he was part of it. The children grew up with prayer happening naturally all round them, with the Bible being as much part of family life as breakfast cereal and bath time. And even if it didn't happen that way in your own home, it did in your friend's round the corner. While the first generation of children was small, we didn't completely realise the preciousness of what we had. We were just busy being church in a new and exciting way and bringing up our families in a way that helped and supported each other. Except that even then, when we went to Spring Harvest and in the leaders' seminars they described what church should be like, we wanted to leap up and shout, 'but ours *is* like that!'

As the children progressed through school, we began to realise just how important the close foundational relationships we had built into their lives were. From the estate the children went to many different schools, both private and state – but came home to play and live together with their church friends. These strong peer structures seem to have been a dominant factor in their growing up into faith of their own. For the children of those idyllic early years, church, family, friends all built into a community in which to live and grow into faith. The strength of what they had protected them as they went out into the dangerous waters of secondary school and university. Even now, the oldest, in their thirties, are still close friends and like nothing better than to get together, remember the old days and compare their own children's development.

Community is important – God knew it when he chose the Israelites and we are rediscovering how important it is. Church is community; a people called together to demonstrate the life of God in their own lives. Open, welcoming homes, where Jesus' life is lived out and shared, are the outworking of that community. The church community must, as we managed to, value the very old and the very young, and everyone in between. Our children were never talked down to, very seldom during this time did we have Sunday school; they contributed to the music for worship; acted, read, and learnt to respect the adults' right to quietness while the sermon was happening. At every level, we tried to show they were an integral and valuable part of the community. Before you think that we must have been an extraordinarily gifted set of people let me assure you that we weren't. We had not been to seminars on how to run family services. We had not all been to Bible College. We were not handpicked in any sense, except by all living in the same area. But we experimented, we learnt, we made mistakes and we had successes. Over the years we got better at what we were doing. And we talked – how we talked, we discussed and prayed about everything. But the secret I think was this. We never expected it *not* to work. We knew God had given us a very special church environment and that he was involved in our community, and that included the children. We had a strong feeling of being in the covenant, and because we did not have any church traditions or experiences to tell us otherwise, we knew that our children, the minute they were born, or even before, were part of God's people in that place. Somehow we learnt to live, as God's people in community in a way I have not seen duplicated anywhere else, though I am sure other churches like that exist.

Maybe it worked this way for us because it was a new church, and it began by meeting in people's homes. Maybe it was because geography became more important than denomination. Maybe it was because we started from scratch and discussed and prayed about everything. Our one 'tradition' was that we had no traditions. Maybe it was because we all lived so close to each other that there was no room for pretence or Sunday-only Christianity. Maybe it was all these things. Maybe it was because we needed to know it could happen, so that later, when many of us have had to move away, the vision is still there. At the time, of course, we did not realise just what we had, but I am so grateful to that church because it gave, not only mine, but all its children, a secure church and home foundation from which to grow into faith – and with only one or two exceptions, they all have.

It was a very special time – and it is not like that now. New vibrant community life has degenerated into traditional church attendance – but we did it once, and the effect on all the children brought up in that environment is amazing. There are several on the mission field, several in church leadership roles, no broken marriages or unholy relationships, and well over 90% over a twenty year period grew up into their own vibrant faith without the trauma of 'wilderness years', including their time away at further education! We trusted and obeyed as well as we could and the Lord blessed them. This may seem simplistic – but faith often is!

It can happen – and it does. I recently heard of another church, again on a housing estate which is growing its kids into both spiritual and physical maturity at the same time. This one is now on its second church plant and they, like us, attribute their success in keeping their teenagers on the 'simple preaching, loving atmosphere, community and unshockability!' that the church managed to live out. I wondered whether there was some significance in the fact that both these churches were on housing estates and I think that the significance is that the housing estate defined a specific geographical limit to the churches influence. We were known throughout the estate as 'the yellow poster people' because all our church publicity, scattered liberally on lampposts and notice boards was on yellow paper. This was throughout, and only throughout the estate.

The Church of England had the right idea years ago when the parish system was invented. One priest for 600 people. A community. Of course now the parishes cover far more people as population density has increased. But the principle works.

It was the same in the Old Testament. Jethro, Moses' father in law had come to visit him in the desert after Moses had led the people out of Egypt. Moses took a little time off to welcome him, but first thing next morning he was back on duty, dealing with all the problems the Israelites brought to him. There were 600,000 of them – the

Israelites, not the problems! So Jethro did not get to see his son in law again till very late that night. So it went on; Moses must have been getting more and more frazzled by all their demands on him. Jethro wisely stepped in and pointed out that Moses could not manage this many people on his own. You would have thought that Moses, having been brought up in the royal palace in Egypt would have learned the art of delegation, but no, he was doing it all himself. Jethro pointed out that he should appoint men as 'officials over thousands, hundreds, fifties and tens'. [Exodus 18] All large people groups need to be broken down into manageable groups, and the people of God are no different. Our little church was part of the greater church of God in Reading; we knew who we were and we knew where the limits of our geographical influence were.

Obviously it is dangerous to argue from the experience of one relatively small church and try to make it work for everyone. But there are things that worked for us, principles that can be taken and applied. The first part of the book looked at the unspoken theology behind our church, and the second section began to work out how we apply this knowledge of God as a covenant keeping God in our family situations. Now we are looking at the outworking of that theology in the church setting, because this underlying theological stance is the reason our church worked the way it did. The first factor which is apparent and which we have begun to discuss is that the church must be a recognisable community within a recognisable community. We were identifiable as 'the yellow poster people'. We were noticeable. We interacted with the community. We modelled a new more open style of community life. We welcomed people dipping in and dipping out.

The church in the West needs as a whole to rediscover this aspect of community in its life. Because at the moment we are failing – failing to reach out to a world that desperately needs God, failing even to keep our own children. Yet there is one thing that we have, that cannot be replicated outside – true community. This is what will keep our children as well as bringing in those from outside. True community cannot happen unless it is inspired and energised by supernatural love – God's love. In a real sense, in those early days, we were a family. We belonged together, shared childcare, shared meals, shared lives. The fact that we lived a community lifestyle affected all those around us. Also and importantly it gave our children a wide range of 'significant adults' who knew them well and who were willing to be involved. It also took the burden off parents who were going through hard times. We had a family where the mother was clinically depressed, but her children did not miss out on parties and outings. We had several families where unemployment meant money was tight for a while, but prayer, friendship and shared meals supported them through. We all cheered when exams were passed and sympathised when they weren't. This all sounds unbearably twee and too good to be true. There were of course arguments, bad times, illnesses, deaths, just as anywhere else. The first time a drum kit was brought in as part of the worship band, a church member walked out! He later became the young drummer's biggest fan, but only after a lot of discussion and prayer and tolerance and willingness to change on everyone's part. Like everyone else, everywhere, we fought and argued, but we also learnt to apologise and forgive and accept each other. You couldn't stay angry with people you were working with every Saturday as you built the church building together and whose children were in and out of your house. For the sake of the church and our witness to those around us the difficulties had to be worked through together and the reality of our faith and our church life together were what helped us to live through them.

The situation of the church as community within community was important but so also was its size. It was both big enough and small enough. We have since said that we were the original cell church before the creation of the concept. Our focus was always on serving and meeting the needs of the community within which we existed. The church ended up with two congregations each Sunday meeting at opposite ends of the estate, because that way we were within walking distance of everyone – a truly local church. As already said, we held most of the meetings in homes scattered around the estate. But we always stayed big enough for interfamily relationships. Many churches now are turning to the cell group model. This is often claimed as 'the answer' for this time. It may be one answer but I think the concept of cells needs to be carefully looked at. One of the alleged advantages of the cell model is that we can make cells 'homogenous' and therefore relevant to the people who belong. Thus we could have a cell for hospital workers or students. But if we divide our churches into work related cells like this or into single generation cells we are losing a very significant dimension of church. Jesus came to break down the divisions, not to reinforce them. Meeting in homogenous groups has value but it cannot be a replacement for intergenerational worship and learning. Several young people, happily involved in their own youth cells, have expressed to me the feeling that they are missing out by not knowing and relating to the older people within their church. One young man said, ' I'd love to have someone who would be a kind of mentor to me – there's so much that I don't know.'

The older people also lose something vital if they are not involved with younger ones. So a church divided into age related cells loses a vital dimension of family life, and neglects the building up of the body. If your teenagers have their own cells, that is fine, as long as there are also teaching and worshipping opportunities with other generations. The older generation has much wisdom and experience that should be shared with the younger ones and the younger ones have enthusiasm and vision. The fact that the generations not only tolerate but also actively enjoy each other's company can have a tremendous effect on people who have never known this within their own families. Within the church community, where the Holy Spirit is active, there is an opportunity to rebuild the strong and healthy intergenerational relationships that are so missing outside the church.

Equally if a cell of twelve of so members is intergenerational then it is surely too small. This is not enough for families. Children, and teenagers in particular, need a peer group. One of the major strengths of our church and a significant factor in most young people's journey safely through their teenage years is a good group of Christian friends. Over and over again when I have asked for factors in keeping teenagers in the church, people have said, 'It was the youth group that kept them here'. But if you are the only teenager in your cell, you are not going to be very keen on going to it.

The good thing that this concept of cell church is doing is focussing attention on the immediate locality of homes and on looking out to the community. But this can also happen, as it did for us, in a small local church. The ideal surely is cell within community. Or families within community. Or community within community as we had.

The church is the result of God's mission to his world. It is the vessel God chose for mission. It comes into being as a result of mission. When it stops being a mission it dies. Its role is to reach out to the world with the message of reconciliation and hope, and to represent the kingdom of God on earth. It is not the Kingdom, but it is the place where kingdom values should be lived out. And its form; cell, community, congregation, or some new form that we haven't seen yet, must be both missionary and demonstration, so the ghetto that so many of us have backed ourselves into is no longer possible as a valid manifestation of church. Church must be community within community. This, for a little while, we managed; it can be done. For the sake of our own children, and the world outside, it must be done more and more.

In my description of the church where my children grew up, there are three main factors which seem to have contributed to the high 'success rate' – community life, peer and adult approval, involvement and affirmation. Because it was a new church, in a socially new situation as well, there were no traditions. We felt that it was important right from the beginning that the children belonged and that they were accepted as part of the community as they were. We also valued, indeed needed their input into church services, children played instruments, read and prayed, acted and even worked the PA system. They were an integral and useful part of the congregation and Sunday by Sunday it was reinforced that they belonged. This adult approval is important; if the children are always taken somewhere different for their teaching there can be no real community, just age groups. Churches that integrate their children and young people seem to have greater success at keeping them. Obviously most young people will also want their own groups, and that too is important as peer pressure plays a great part in their development, but the sense of being linked into the adult church, if missing, is a factor in many not continuing with church attendance into their adult years.

When the whole church congregation, not just the youth leaders, cares about the young people, then the young people stay in the church. There was a very old lady in our church who had been a missionary in India for most of her life. She wore smart tweed skirts and twin sets and wound her long grey hair into an elegant bun. You would have thought that she had nothing in common with the young people of today. Yet she was the most popular visitor of all among the young men at the drug rehabilitation centre we were involved in. Why? Because she would go for long leisurely walks with the young men around the grounds and listen to them. They told Doc Ruth things about their lives, their girlfriends, their hopes, their childhoods, that no on else ever heard. All because she had time to go for a walk with them. We are hearing increasingly that children are not like they used to be – they are more demanding, more sure of themselves, more sophisticated, more materialistic. In many ways they are. But, as these young recovering drug addicts showed they are still completely lost without God, and it is love that can bring them closer to him. Love, like this, shown by the most unexpected members of their church community.

In our new community church there was not one family that expected the children to fall out of the church, as they became teenagers. They were kept by the community's love and prayer and modelling and faith. They were probably not even aware of this. They were just too busy having fun, organising the younger ones, going to Spring Harvest, taking services, playing music, inviting their friends to youth group, finding out about God and enjoying their families and friends' families to even think about rebelling. God was a real part of their lives and as they grew up they took this family faith for their own.

It is possible but only if we take God at his word and believe and obey. The expectations of the families that make up the church community are inextricably bound up with the expectations and goals of the church. If the whole community is committed to holy living, that will inevitably affect the corporate life of the church as well as the life of the individual members. If the church leaders are convinced that the teenagers need not rebel, that they are able to be used by God and to see him use them, that intergenerational love is fundamental to being the people of God, then they will preach and teach and model it and arrange the church so that it happens. But if they sit back and wait for the teenagers to return as adults after years of wandering, they are in for a great disappointment, as well as shrinking numbers. If they have a thriving youth work which is totally unrelated to the rest of the church, I believe that those young people are still in danger, but that the falling away will come at a later age.

Our expectations, either church or family, affect the future. We need to make sure our expectations of our young people are in line with what God wants for them, and do all we can to make these expectations into really in our home life and in our church life. But even then, we may find God expands or overturns those expectations.

Chapter Thirteen

Churches that Work

In the Middle Ages in England church attendance Sunday by Sunday was expected – even legislated for. It you did not go you were likely to be fined! Of course what went on inside the head when the service was in incomprehensible Latin could not be legislated for, but the churches were full! Churchgoing fulfilled a need and a duty in those days. These days many churches are not only not full, but may have been converted into private homes, mosques or, as in Reading town centre, bookshops! Is this symptomatic that church going is no longer seen as either a need or a duty, or even a pleasure these days? And yet as the previous chapter shows, sometimes and in some places it works, and churches remain full, even growing. It seems that just as, within our families our expectations have a lot to do with whether the children to grow up smoothly into faith, so in churches our expectations and the way we work towards them can facilitate or hinder not just the young people's growth but also the continued existence of the church as a healthy growing entity.

But so often, in church life, we seem to start out well and then 'lose the plot'. We see churches where God did great things, but now they are empty, or aging. And the Spirit moves elsewhere. Yet Jesus said that he would build his church and the gates of hell would not prevail against it. Our covenant-making God is committed to generations serving him; the old time church builders believed it when they spent years and years creating beautiful ornate stone buildings as a place to worship God. If they had not believed in his commitment to them and theirs to him, they would not have spent so much time and effort on places where he can be worshipped. God is faithful – he is committed to generation after generation of people serving him. And yet all around us churches are shrinking. Their congregations are ageing. As we have seen the statistics tell us that this generation may well be the last. The haemorrhage is getting life threatening. How, in an increasingly impersonal society do we stop it happening? The church in the west is in crisis. There is an ongoing debate about what new forms of church we need if we are to exist. Old formats have been tried and found wanting. Something radical does need to be done. The question is what? One thing that is for sure is that there is no one format which fits every situation. Church in the inner city will be significantly different from church in a village. Unless we become relevant, we will die.

But there are clues to all this. The structures that have been set out in this book as benefiting the next generation would seem to be the very answers that would benefit the church. Building community is vital – for the children and for the church. How we do that may be in a million different ways, depending on context.

God's people the Jews lived in community – they were the people of God. So church needs to be first and foremost a community of worshipping people. But it needs to be a real community – there is no community in just saying we are a family, when our only contact is once or twice on Sundays. Even dividing the church into cells does not help if that is no more than a once a week meeting, or if our cells only operate on a horizontal line. As church leaders and parents, we have to work out a way that works, not just for one generation, but also for succeeding generations.

There are churches where life has gone on for generations; one such is Greyfriars church in Reading. It was known as a lively church in the fifties and before and is still a thriving church community. One family, for example, had a great uncle, who was a churchwarden there, in the years before the Second World War. Then the father was the organist for many years and the son grew up in the church. Now he has watched his own children grow into adulthood and faith in the same church in a peaceful and unrebellious way just as he himself did. According to this father, the secret that Greyfriars Church learnt was similar to what this book has all been about. Children and young people have always been valued and appreciated. There is a lively sense of being the people of God. The church, though actually situated in the centre of Reading makes sure its scattered congregation is divided into home groups big enough to provide support for the young people as well as providing exciting and challenging activities. The church has an expectation that its young people will come through into faith and the whole church prays and works to that end. Always in the forefront of this church's thinking is that they are willing to change and to spend to meet the needs of their families and young people. The church has a tradition of sending the teenagers off to do mission work both in this country and overseas. Intergenerational relationships are seen as important and to be valued and nurtured. Being a town centre church with no natural 'parish boundary' within which its members live, the leadership has always within its view the need to build community. They do this by a strong and active system of home groups, arranged geographically, they have a church centre where the whole church family comes for various activities but also to serve the community together, young people included, they provide opportunities for the youth to be involved in the worshipping life of the church but also to go and do creative things together as a group, and they actively encourage overseas experience, working with the youth to raise funds if needed. Faith in God about the next generation, shared within a community setting, faith in their young people and a faith *for* their young people that is more challenging and exciting than anything else in their lives. God honours this, and the haemorrhage, at least in this situation, does not occur.

Both churches and families have expectations about what will happen to the young people in their care. By consideration of various Biblical themes within this book it becomes apparent that there is hope. Churches do not have to live with the expectation that our teenage population will dwindle and disappear. We, as parents, do not have to expect our children to abandon God and hope against hope that they will return at some time in the future. Lively Spirit filled community churches do not inevitably transform themselves into clubs for like-minded people. Churches should also have the expectation that their young people are inheritors of the blessings which come as a result of our obedience.

But we do not see this; the lifeblood is draining away from the church. We are always so eager not to apportion blame, to assure parents of rebellious children that it is not their fault and the children will return to the fold. As we have seen, at the beginning of this book, the statistics tell a different story. We are responsible for our children's behaviour. If we, as church or family, have neglected their spiritual well being we need to face up to that fact and repent. Not to blame, because it might be that it was unwitting or through lack of understanding or knowledge or teaching or faith.

But together, in an attempt to stop the haemorrhage, we must begin to work out how Christianity affects all of everyday life, to think through the implications of faith in the twenty-first century, and to find a God-honouring way in a society that is determined to go in the other direction. But we have to do something about all this. For the sake of the next generation. For the sake of the ones who are drifting unnoticed away from the church and those who, with very little encouragement, would drift *in* through the doors and start to belong and change and believe. We have something worth sharing; we have something worth living. But we are still hiding it. So churches, not just families within churches, need to reassess their expectations and their commitment to radical, exciting living.

We are all inheritors of church traditions which have their own effects on our own life of faith as well as making the successful transmission of radical and committed faith down the generations more or less likely. If the families within the church transform themselves into the open, faithful and committed people that I have been saying we need to be, the churches may find that they have to seriously reconsider the format of services and the structures they put in place for their people because the life of their congregations will move out from the place of worship and into daily life.

God tells us he is committed to the children of his servants and that they will inherit the land. Our family traditions can help or hinder this process. Our church traditions can help or hinder this process. Throughout this book my argument has been that if we see the depth of God's commitment to us, the power of his desire to have a covenant people for himself, his impulse towards community reaching downwards and outwards; if we respond with our whole lives living in holiness and openness to him and to each other, then we will find that Jesus is irresistible to our teenagers. They will see in him somebody glorious and exciting and challenging because that's what he is. They will have seen enough so that when things get tough they will stick with it and work through the doubt. Dostoievski expressed his own faith like this; 'It is not as a child that I believe and confess

Christ. My hosanna is born of a furnace of doubt.' If they see that reality in their church and home life as they grow up, the furnace will refine, not destroy, their commitment to the Lord.

Things had been going really well, but the 'furnace of doubt' was approaching. The disciples looked at all the crowds following Jesus and were really excited. So many people listening to his every word. They had seen Jesus turn one little boy's supper into a feast for thousands, they had seen him walking on water, and they thought he was on the way to general acclaim and fame. But then he started talking about strange things, eating his flesh and drinking his blood, and the crowds began fading away. This was too much for good Jews who never ate anything with blood in it. They couldn't, God had forbidden it. Now here was Jesus making these disgusting claims. Soon there were only his faithful few left. 'You do not want to leave too, do you?' Jesus asked. Simon Peter, without a moment's hesitation replied for them all, 'Lord, to whom shall we go? You have the words of eternal life.' [John 6:67-68].

He still does. Many other voices are calling us and our young people. There are hard things that Jesus will demand of us. Following him will require changes in our thinking, even a radical shift of worldview. He may take us into difficult places and demand impossible things. Life may be more conformist, more comfortable without him. But only Jesus can give us eternal life – life of the same kind and same quality that God has.

Chapter Fourteen

The Way Forward

As I come to the end of writing this book I am quite amazed to discover that what I appear to have been doing is exploring the implications of covenant theology. But according to my dictionary theology is only an explanation of the way that God works in human experience and previous to being theology this book was experience – lived out in the life of my family and many others that I know. The theology followed life. All I can say is that it works. It worked for me. It worked for my church. What you make of it is up to you. You can retreat behind denominational 'walls' – 'well that's all right for her but it's not what my church believes'. I appreciate that we all interpret the Bible in our own way and so it is perfectly possible that you will be able to find proofs that the Bible provides texts which 'let you off the hook'? Or are you going to look at society for reasons not to believe or act on what you have read?

We all know we have made mistakes. No one is a perfect parent. No church gets it right all the time either. But if the church haemorrhages to death, it can only be our fault. We have seen that the lifeblood flowing away is the younger generation. The 'missing generation' in the church is getting wider. The twenties and thirties are largely missing. The teenagers are missing and the preteens are going. Apportioning blame is never a good way forward. It has been my contention that church and family belong together and need each other. No one or two adults can be all a child needs. We all need community, but the children, particularly those of single parents or dysfunctional families, need it most. All of us together need to reclaim the faith that God is committed to a continuing church and to our next generation. It may be that closing the generation gap is the way to heal the church.

We must stop this haemorrhage. Haemorrhage is a very strange way to die. A slow haemorrhage can go unnoticed for a long time, except for anaemia leading to a tendency to weakness, tiredness and increased susceptibility to infection. But a swift haemorrhage though it may be painful at the time of rupture, can be a very peaceful, painless way to die as the brain is starved of oxygen and feelings shut down. But either way death is the ultimate result unless serious intervention occurs. Many people have likened the state of the church in the West to the last stages of a serious haemorrhage. Intervention is necessary. This book is true – it is based on things that actually happened and people who actually exist and are walking strongly and faithfully with their God throughout their childhood and adult lives.

There is in our church a family who have all been committed Christians for at least five generations. The only factor that seems to make any sense of why this has happened is simply that it was expected. The parents of each new generation wanted, prayed and worked for it. They never envisaged anything other than faith for each new generation. As we have already found, in the Bible, God is far more committed to each new generation than we are. But we have to believe it. This family did, and the youngest member of it, little six-year-old Suzanna has the joy of meeting aunts, great-aunts and uncles, granny and granddad, and great grandma whenever she comes to church. For her, family is so bound up with church that there can be very little distinction between home and church. No one expects her to abandon her family faith any more than they expect her to turn her back on her other family ties as she grows up. The expectation is that she too will grow up into the Lord. Four generations of her own family are praying that this will be so. The Lord promises that he will keep his covenant to a thousand generations of those who love him and keep his commandments. I think Suzanna is safe!

God's purpose is to build his church – historically and generationally as well as numerically. His mission is to redeem the world, and the church has to be involved in that mission. The church is not meant to be a one-generation, dying thing. We are meant to build the church both out into segments of society that do not know about the truth and the freedom that Jesus brings, and also inwards to bequeath that truth and that freedom and that life downwards in our own families, to our children and their children. The devil has no right to sneak in and snatch our children out. Throughout history in its various manifestations the family has continued to exist and adapt, handing genes, languages and traditions down from generation to generation. In the church too, life is handed down, as shown in the history of the people of Israel, and of the church throughout the ages until this last generation, so that the children and grandchildren of believers grow up into the faith, becoming believers themselves. Each generation should hand the baton on to the next. There are plentiful promises in God's word that he will bless and save the children of his servants; that his favour does continue from generation to generation. It does work. He made the promises, we trusted him and did our best to obey the commands, and he blessed. It was a joint church and family thing, together we all believed God for the future of all our children. We should expect God to keep his promises about the children of believers; we expect him to keep his other promises. But has the church forgotten these promises? In many places it seems that all that is expected for children these days is rebellion and that they will slip away from the church; no wonder so many children of Christian parents are not making it through. We don't expect them to, and so we do very little to stop the haemorrhage happening. We have to make promises in our turn; promises that whatever happens we will trust God with our children, promises that we will do all we can, as individuals and as church to enable them to grow smoothly and without trauma into faith. Let us take God at his word again; the word that says he will give our children the land, that he will bless our children if we honour and obey him, and let us watch him build the church in our homes and communities in the next generation. Then we will see the haemorrhaging stop because the young people will realise that being part of God's covenant community is the most exciting place in the world to be.

When my daughter finished school she went to America with YWAM for a gap year. She had gained good A level results and had her university place waiting for her when she came home. Halfway through her time there she phoned to say that she was not coming back to university but wanted to stay and do a second year with YWAM, and then remain part of the organisation. Her father spent a couple of days pacing the house muttering. 'We didn't spend all that money on her education just so she could...' and 'What a waste of her brainpower...' and 'She won't get a job without a degree'. We had trusted God with her future, but didn't like it when he took her down a different, and more unusual path than the one we expected for her. But at last we agreed that she had to make her own decisions, and we had to trust her and God to know what course her life should take. And we learnt for ourselves what we knew in theory – God really does have a plan for each and every life he creates, and it is different from what we would plan. At every stage of our children's lives we expect them to do certain things in certain ways and when they don't we are taken aback. Expectations can be good and liberating, or they can be bad and restricting. We have already seen that children will behave in the way they are expected to and if you tell a child it is naughty, it will become more and more badly behaved. 'Catch them being clever, catch them being good' is a useful motto for teachers and parents alike. If we expect our children to fall away from God, to be rebellious and uncommunicative, then they will be. But if we expect them to grow up into faith they will – even if as in our case, that faith then leads them along paths we had not planned out for them.

A young couple I know were asked by non Christian friends how they had the courage to get married, how they could possibly commit to each other for life. Their response; 'We just know – it's going to be for ever'. Their expectation was that they would go on loving each other for the rest of their lives, and their intention was to do all they could, with God's help, to ensure that they did. Any commitment is a risk – faith in a marriage partner is surely more of a risk than faith in an almighty God! But faith grows as we put it to the test, one step at a time. We need a bit more of this in our expectations for our children and their children. God is committed to them forever – he says so – so why should we ever think that they would fall away or turn their backs on him. Gwyn, 80 years old, and Suzanna's great grandma, said of her family that faith was 'in the genes'. Obviously she did not mean that in a literal sense but there is a spiritual truth – what we put in, what God puts in, will come out. If their surroundings, at home and at church, are such that Jesus is real, exciting, and challenging, and the people who inhabit those surroundings are genuine, holy and committed, and also real, exciting and challenging, there is very little in earth or heaven that will be able to tear them away from him. Real sold out, lived out Christianity is contagious!

So what are our expectations for our teenagers? Well, the sky is the limit. But the choice is ours. Do you remember the spies who went into the land of Israel? Ten of them saw the powerful occupants, the weapons, the fortified towns, and said God could not possibly get them into the land. Two saw the grapes and the honey and the rich pastureland and praised God for his provision for his people. And they got exactly what they saw! The ten died in the desert; the two entered the land with the children forty years later. It's the same for us. We get what we see. You can look at what is going on in society and let that blind you to the truth of God's word. Or you can believe his word, rely on his promises, work towards his kingdom and see what he can do in churches and families that take him at his word.

Throughout this book we have used various metaphors to explain what is happening to our children and young people – they are haemorrhaging away, they are wandering in the wilderness, they are the lost generation. Exodus, as used in the title, is a double-sided word. It just means leaving. Leaving the bad, and heading for the better, or leaving the good and heading out into the wilderness. The Israelites leaving Egypt saw it as a wonderful thing, even though most of them just wandered in the desert until they died. The young people are leaving what they see as bondage. They are 'in exodus', looking for their promised land. We don't have to watch them go – there is no other promised land for them but the one God gives. Just as Moses had to work at persuading the leaders of the Israelites that what he said came from God, we may need to work at persuading ourselves and our churches that the children can be brought into the Promised Land. Like, them, we need to be convinced that it is possible. I am convinced; are you?

The Israelites, standing on the brink of the Promised Land were given instructions by Moses for remembering how they were to behave. Half the Israelites – six tribes, were to stand on Mount Gerizim and proclaim the blessings that come from obedience, while the other six tribes stood on Mount Ebal and shouted curses – the result of disobedience. One side proclaimed life, the other death. The Israelites were told to choose which they wanted. There is a similar choice today. The statistics tell us the church is dying. Statistically it cannot survive. We cannot expect the next generation to come into the Kingdom. We only have to turn on the news or open the newspaper to hear the curses echoing in our ears. But when we read God's word the promises shout of his blessing for us and for the next generations. But the choice is ours. There is no way our children will learn the truth about God if we don't teach them; school won't, society won't, peers won't nor will other adults. Satan is fighting to destroy the family; he hates family because faithful Christian families are a vivid picture of the faithful loving God whom he wants to defeat. He has just about won the battle outside the church and he wants to get us on the run too. We need to wake up to what is happening and claim the next generation back for God. The church should be prophetic for the world; Satan is battling for the hearts and minds of the next generation and so far he hasn't had to fight very hard. Christian families must fight back and become a light to the world – radically different and living life God's way; showing that it can be done – if God does it!

Jesus' coming was supremely an act of reconciliation; he reconciled us to God, and to each other. He broke down, and is still breaking down, the barriers of race, colour and class – 'there is now neither Jew nor Greek, slave nor free, male nor female, for you` are all one in Christ Jesus.' [Galatians 3:28]. And the last gap he came to close was the generation gap – this gap that we have invented in the last century, otherwise Paul might well have included it in his list of reconciliations!

We have a wonderful opportunity to change the climate – to work as church leaders and as parents to show the world that true intergenerational community is alive and well in God's kingdom and nowhere else. Extinction is not necessary; I don't think it is even possible. Jesus said, 'I will build my church and the gates of hell will not prevail against it'. So we can once again see the church full of young vibrant life. But it's up to us. It is a corporate, yet individual responsibility. I don't want to be part of a church that feebly holds a sticking plaster over a burst artery. I want to be part of a church that responds with surgery, transfusions, whatever is needed to stop the haemorrhage and bring health and growth again. So I imagine do you. And so, I venture to ask, what are you going to do about it? My children are part of that church, living exciting challenging lives with their exciting challenging God. Yours can be too. Together we can stop the haemorrhage!